Liberty in the Balance

FOUNDATIONS OF AMERICAN GOVERNMENT AND POLITICAL SCIENCE

Joseph P. Harris, Consulting Editor

Revisions and additions have been made to keep this series up to date and to enlarge its scope, but its purpose remains the same as it was on first publication: To provide a group of relatively short treatises dealing with major aspects of government in modern society. Each volume introduces the reader to a major field of political science through a discussion of important issues, problems, processes, and forces and includes at the same time an account of American political institutions. The author of each work is a distinguished scholar who specializes in and teaches the subjects covered. Together the volumes are well adapted to serving the needs of introductory courses in American government and political science.

Since Andrew Hacker's volume covers material of an essentially timeless nature only minor corrections have been made for the new printing. The notation, second edition, identifies other volumes that have been more extensively revised. The greatest expansion of material occurred in the revision which turned The President and Congress *by Rowland Egger and Joseph P. Harris into two books separately discussing the Presidency and the Congress. The authors and the editor have agreed that for the time being revision of* Public Administration in Modern Society *should be deferred.*

ANDREW HACKER: The Study of Politics: The Western Tradition and American Origins

C. HERMAN PRITCHETT: The American Constitutional System, 2D ED.

HUGH A. BONE and AUSTIN RANNEY: Politics and Voters, 2D ED.

ROWLAND EGGER: The President of the United States

JOSEPH P. HARRIS: Congress and the Legislative Process

(The two books listed above were revised and enlarged from materials contained in the first edition of *The President and Congress* by Rowland Egger and Joseph P. Harris.)

JOHN J. CORSON and JOSEPH P. HARRIS: Public Administration in Modern Society

CHARLES O. LERCHE, JR.: America in World Affairs, 2D ED.

CHARLES R. ADRIAN: Governing Our Fifty States and Their Communities, 2D ED.

H. FRANK WAY, JR.: Liberty in the Balance: Current Issues in Civil Liberties, 2D ED.

LIBERTY IN THE BALANCE

Current Issues in Civil Liberties

H. Frank Way, Jr.

Associate Professor of Political Science
University of California, Riverside

McGRAW-HILL BOOK COMPANY
NEW YORK / ST. LOUIS / SAN FRANCISCO
TORONTO / LONDON / SYDNEY

LIBERTY IN THE BALANCE:
Current Issues in Civil Liberties

Robert Frost quotation (p. 128) from "Stopping by Woods on a Snowy Evening" from
Complete Poems of Robert Frost. Copyright
1923 by Holt, Rinehart and Winston, Inc.
Copyright renewed 1951 by Robert Frost.
Reprinted by permission of Holt, Rinehart
and Winston, Inc.

1234567890(MR)72106987

*This book is set in linotype Janson. The orig-
inal specimen sheets date from about 1700 and
are of Dutch origin.*

Preface

It is the common fate of the indolent to see their rights become a prey to the active. The condition upon which God hath given liberty to man is eternal vigilance; which condition if he break, servitude is at once the consequence of his crime and the punishment of his guilt.

John P. Curran, 1790

The words of John Curran are as timely for this generation as they were for the 1790s. Yet a recognition of the importance of eternal vigilance does not solve the conundrum posed to each generation: where and how must we be vigilant?

Each day in some city council room, or in a legislative body, or in a police station the liberty of free men will weigh in the balance. Each day decisions are made, policies adopted, actions taken which can narrow the scope of human freedom. All too frequently when liberty is in the balance the attention of free men is focused elsewhere. The climate of public indifference to the "petty" invasions of liberty, to the "minor" violations of justice, carries with it the winds of tyranny—petty and colossal. Freedom is never secure where a people are indifferent to the banning of a book in the local public library, the firing of a school teacher for participating in a peace march, or the quiet gerrymandering of a school district in order to exclude Negroes.

But even when local opinion is raised against the invasions of liberty the frequent conclusion is that such issues should be solved by lawyers and judges. Yet liberty is not essentially a legal matter. Liberty is an integral part of the politics of citizenship and the forum for its preservation is not just in a court of law; the first forum is the library board meeting, the city council meeting, the party precinct meeting, the picket line, or the sit-in. As the late Mr. Justice

Jackson once observed, ". . . the attitude of a society and of its organized political forces rather than its legal machinery, is the controlling force in the character of free institutions." Nonetheless, as the reader will discover in the following chapters, Americans have an unhealthy deference to a legalistic solution to the current issues in civil liberties.

In the Preface to the first edition of this book I noted that the civil liberties scene in the United States is far from static. There have been significant changes in every major topic treated in this book since it first appeared. While I have attempted to take these changes into consideration in this edition, it is virtually impossible to keep pace with some issues, for example, civil rights. It is equally difficult to write about current issues without excluding issues which are not only timely but of vital importance. What is attempted in this book is not to survey every current issue but rather to select a few important ones and to study each in some depth. The topics selected for analysis are more than current issues—they are recurrent issues in liberty. Something the reader will undoubtedly discover for himself is that my analysis is not always without bias. I hope, however, that the only bias is in favor of freedom.

H. Frank Way

Contents

RACE DISCRIMINATION: "WE SHALL OVERCOME"

Chapter 1

GO HOME, FREEDOM

You, Albany Nigger, are black, your hair is kinky, you smell like greens and side pork, you shuffle after white men, lust for his women folk, you live in Harlem town and you are getting damned uppity with your demonstrations and your prayer meetings. Your demands are an outrage—to worship at a white man's church, to sit next to white women at the movies, to eat with white folks and to go to school with white children. Nigger, you are making revolution! You and your agitator friends from the North with your sit-ins, registration drives, and praying! Nigger, didn't you hear them tell that black boy of yours "Go Home, Freedom"?

THE ALBANY MOVEMENT

Albany, Georgia, is located in Dougherty County on the fringe of the Georgia Black Belt. It is the principal trade center for southwestern Georgia. Albany is a city of over 55,000 souls, with textile and thread mills, pecan, peanut, meat packing, and food-processing plants. It is a bustling little city, proud of its growth and confident of its future. The local chamber of commerce calls it the "city of opportunity" and lists its most valuable asset as a remarkable community spirit; indeed, "no city has a spirit of cooperation more fully developed." The city is proud of its churches, its palm-lined Broad Avenue, its new high school; it is proud of the Phoebe-Putney Hospital, of the Radium Springs, and of Tift Park with its ultramodern pool. But Albany— that is, white Albany—the city of opportunity, is not very proud of 40 per cent of its population, because 40 per cent of Albany, the Harlem district Negroes, have been in revolt since 1961. The Negroes have demanded recognition as equal citizens in Albany; they want to be able to shop freely on Broad Avenue, to receive equal treatment in the Phoebe-Putney Hospital, to swim in the Tift Park pool, and to attend integrated public schools.

"A DAMN NIGGER" William Hansen, a young white man from Cincinnati, came to Albany in the summer of 1962 to work for the Student Non-Violent Coordinating Committee. On the afternoon of July 25, the Reverend Martin Luther King led a small group to the city hall to attempt to talk to the city commission. The police arrested Dr. King and his followers for "disturbing the peace." Later that same afternoon William Hansen accompanied a small group of students to the city hall where they knelt in prayer on the sidewalk to protest Dr. King's arrest. Again Police Chief Laurie Pritchett ordered the demonstrators arrested. After weeks of arrests the city jail was full and William Hansen was sent to the Dougherty County jail in Albany. A deputy sheriff placed Hansen in a cell and remarked to a prison trustee, "This is one of those guys who came down to straighten us out." The prison trustee attacked Hansen and beat him unconscious. Hansen's jaw was broken, his lip split, and several ribs cracked. Three days later C. B. King, the first and only Negro attorney in Albany, attempted to make an inquiry about Hansen's condition. For his effort he was beaten over the head with a walking stick and informed that he was "a damn nigger." [1]

[1] Howard Zinn, *Albany: A Study in National Responsibility*, Southern Regional Council, Atlanta, Ga., 1962, pp. 12–13.

The story of the Albany Movement is in part the story of the second Reconstruction, of the latest desperate attempt by the Negro in Albany and across the nation to secure freedom. The battle has been occasionally marred by violence, but the remarkable feature has been the nonviolent nature of the protest movement. Yet the restraint shown by a man like C. B. King cannot be expected to last indefinitely. The Negro has been turning the other cheek for decades, but the cup of endurance is running out.

The Albany Movement began in the fall of 1961 under the leadership of a group of local middle-class Negroes, inspired by Martin Luther King's Southern Christian Leadership Conference and prodded into action by young local Negroes in the Student Non-Violent Coordinating Committee. The Movement was a forerunner of the Negro urban revolt in the South and North. It was later replaced on the front pages of the nation's press by Birmingham, Oxford, Greenwood, Cambridge, Los Angeles, and New York. By the middle of 1963 the Albany Movement had made few concrete accomplishments. Approximately 1,500 Negroes had been arrested in sit-ins and demonstrations. The sit-ins and demonstrations continued and so did the arrests. All that had been achieved in Albany was the integration of the bus terminal and "vertical integration" of the public library. Local whites remained intransigent to change. In March, 1963, the city commission did repeal all segregation ordinances—not to aid desegregation but in order to make segregation less vulnerable to legal attack. As Police Chief Laurie Pritchett said with a smile to a reporter a few days after the repeal, "You look around and see if anything's integrated, and if it is, call me, will you?" But while the Albany Movement was unable to secure justice for the Negroes in Albany it did for a few months focus national attention on the race issue and made the Negro more conscious of the power of direct action. Albany begot Birmingham, and the impact of Birmingham on the Federal government may ultimately bring justice to the Negroes in Albany.

EDUCATION AND DESEGREGATION

In 1954 in *Brown v. Topeka Board of Education* the United States Supreme Court struck down the "separate but equal doctrine," a doctrine which had not merely upheld segregated public schools, but a doctrine which provided a legal justification for Jim Crowism—racial segregation by custom and law. The Court concluded that governmental segregation on the basis of race was inherently unequal treatment and thus in violation of the provision in the Fourteenth Amendment that no state shall deny any person the "equal protection of the laws." Previously the Court had justified the separation of Negroes and whites by state law in public facilities and education, but had demanded that the separate education facilities be equal. In the *Brown* case the physical plant facilities, curricula, and teachers were equal. The Court, however, considered the intangible factors, concluding that:

> . . . to separate [children] from others of similar age and qualifications solely because of their race generates a feeling of inferiority as to their status in the community that may affect their hearts and minds in a way unlikely ever to be undone.[2]

Realizing the monumental nature of its decision the Court waited until 1955 to hand down the final desegregation order. It did not require immediate compliance but rather instructed the Federal district courts to consider a variety of factors which might affect integration, and then ordered desegregation of local school districts "with all deliberate speed." [3] Eleven years later in the state of Georgia and in the city of Albany the deliberation was only beginning. There has been no speed.

Public education in Albany and in Dougherty County is still largely segregated. There has been little "good faith compliance" by local authorities. Under a Federal court order Albany began desegregation in the fall of 1964. By the end of the 1965–1966 academic year 177 Negro children were attending integrated classes.

In the year of the *Brown* decision, 1954, 18 Southern and border states and the District of Columbia had public education segregation laws. While these laws were in effect declared unconstitutional in 1954 the overwhelming majority of Negro students in these states continue to attend racially segregated and generally inferior schools. With the exception of Tennessee and Arkansas, the border states and the District of Columbia proceeded with desegregation with some reasonable speed. By the beginning of the 1965–1966 school year 6 per cent of the Negro school population in the 11 Southern states were at-

---

[2] *Brown v. Topeka Board of Education*, 347 U.S. 492, 494 (1954).
[3] 349 U.S. 294 (1955).

tending integrated schools. In the border states and the District of Columbia the percentage was 69.

JUDICIAL DESEGREGATION   Desegregation under the *Brown* decision has always had a limited impact primarily because it was instituted and implemented without congressional support and largely without executive support. For many years after the decision neither Congress nor the President gave it their moral or political support. Indeed, the reason the United States Supreme Court was initially able to hand down such a decision can be attributed to the prior inability of the political branches of government to cope with the issue of racial discrimination. A federal system with separated powers and weak national parties is an open invitation to the judiciary to play a larger policy role than would be possible or desirable in a government with a more centralized political power structure. Nevertheless, the ability of the judiciary to implement a highly controversial decision is at best a poor substitute for concerted government action by the major political branches of government.

While there is no question that racial segregation by public authority is illegal, still a court decision is binding only on the immediate litigants in a case. In our legally conscious society, when a higher court indicates a new path in the law there is an expectation that this will be followed by all affected groups. But the South, bitterly objecting to the *Brown* decision, elected to await individual desegregation suits filed by Negro parents in particular school districts, rather than desegregate by executive-legislative action in advance of such litigation. Thus the judicial solution to racial discrimination is an *ad hoc* approach and has afforded segregationists in the North and South their greatest weapon in fighting integration: time, the weapon of doing nothing. In 1963, nine years after the *Brown* decision, only 7.9 per cent of the Negro students in the South and border states were attending integrated public schools. Some border states and the District of Columbia did voluntarily desegregate immediately after the *Brown* decision, but in most areas of high Negro population the white-dominated school boards have ignored the *Brown* decision. In face of such school board inaction, the local Negro must assume the onus and the financial burden of securing a court order for that which is his by right.

Judicial desegregation places a heavy burden on the Negro. The Albany Movement requested desegregation of the public schools in

Dougherty County and Albany and the request was denied. Nineteen Negro students sought to enter the white schools in Albany in September, 1962. They were turned away by the chief of police. Late in 1962 the Federal Department of Justice requested the Dougherty County school board to provide integrated education for the children of military personnel at nearby Turney Air Force Base and the Marine Corps Supply Center. The county received over $500,000 in 1962 from the Federal government under the Federal school aid program to areas impacted by the children of Federal employees stationed at nearby Federal installations. In January, 1963, the board voted unanimously to continue segregation. The failure to achieve voluntary desegregation forced the leaders of the Albany Movement to file a desegregation suit in the Federal district court in 1963.

The judicial approach has the additional limitation of placing a heavy burden on the Federal district courts and Federal courts of appeals. Except for the initial desegregation in 1954–1955 in a few border states and the District of Columbia, most integration has been undertaken by the Federal court order or the immediate threat of a court order. Also, the Federal district judges in the South are by no means unanimous in their support of the desegregation suits. There have been long delays in these suits which can be attributed to a lack of sympathy on the bench for integration. While Federal district judges are appointed by the President, the United States senators of each state play an important if not decisive role in the President's choice of appointees. In 1962 President Kennedy appointed a supporter of Senator Herman Talmadge to the Federal court for the middle district of Georgia. Judge Elliott, former chairman of the Georgia Democratic Central Committee, was at the time of his appointment in 1962 an ardent segregationist. And Elliott hid that fact from no one. In 1952 he was quoted as stating "I don't want these pinks, radicals, and black voters to out-vote those who are trying to preserve our segregation laws and other traditions."

During the crucial summer of 1962 Federal District Judge Elliott issued an injunction against racial protest demonstrations in Albany. The decision was perhaps one of the strangest ever handed down by a Federal court in a civil rights battle. It reasoned that the Federal civil rights statutes were being violated not by the local authorities but rather by the Negro demonstrators! The Albany Movement had to appeal the injunction to the United States Fifth Circuit Court of

Appeals. Appellate Judge Elbert Tuttle revoked the temporary injunction and reminded his colleague that the civil rights statutes were intended to protect individuals from state action and not the opposite. In February, 1963, Judge Elliott dismissed the suit by the leaders of the Albany Movement to desegregate certain public facilities. Again it was necessary for the Negroes to seek redress in the court of appeals.[4] In August, 1961, the city of Albany requested a permanent injunction against demonstrations in Judge Elliott's court. While Judge Elliott finally dismissed the request, he kept it under advisement for several months before making a decision. When Attorney General Robert Kennedy was questioned in April, 1963, about Presidential appointments to the Federal bench in the South he was quoted as saying "I'm very proud of the judges that have been appointed." When queried in particular about Judge Elliott he said his comments also applied to that judge.[5]

Judge Elliott is by no means atypical. In 1963 Federal District Judge Frank M. Scarlett, a Truman appointee, in a suit to desegregate the Savannah, Georgia, schools, ruled against the Negroes after he had allowed testimony to be introduced purporting to prove that Negro children are intellectually inferior to white children and that integration would injure both: "All the evidence before this court was to the effect that difference in test results between the white and Negro students is attributable in large part to heredity factors. . . ." Again Judge Elbert Tuttle overruled the lower court and reminded Judge Scarlett that "the district court for the Southern District of Georgia is bound by the decisions of the U.S. Supreme Court, as we are. . . ." Judge Tuttle ordered integration of at least one grade in the Savannah schools by the fall of 1963.

The fact that some Federal judges have allowed the states to evade and delay in integration does not mean that the Federal judiciary is to be condemned for its role in desegregation. On the contrary, the Federal judiciary deserves a great deal of credit for the integration that has been achieved. When state governors and legislatures were offering massive resistance, interposition, and in the case of Little Rock and Oxford, even physical force to resist integration, the Federal judiciary continued to act as a legal forum for the redress of Negro grievances. If nothing else, the Federal judiciary and in particular the Supreme Court focused national attention on a grievous problem which

---

[4] *Anderson v. Kelly*, 32 F.R.D. 355 (1963).
[5] *The New York Times*, Apr. 27, 1963, Western ed., p. 4.

no other agency of the government was either willing or able to consider.

THE DESEGREGATION CHARADE   The Supreme Court said in the Little Rock case in 1958 [6] that:

> . . . . delay in any guise in order to deny the constitutional rights of Negro children could not be countenanced and that only a prompt start, diligently and earnestly pursued, to eliminate racial segregation from the public schools could constitute good faith compliance. State authorities were thus duty bound to devote every effort toward initiating desegregation. . . .

The Court also noted that state support of racially segregated schools ". . . through any arrangement, management, funds, or property cannot be squared with the . . . command that no state shall deny to any person within its jurisdiction the equal protection of the laws." In spite of the rulings of the Supreme Court, however, the Southern states set about defeating desegregation by a game of legal charades.

Integration has been avoided in the South by a variety of tactics, some subtle and some not. Immediately after the *Brown* decision, when reaction in the South was at its highest pitch, many states, spurred on by the new White Citizens' Councils movement, adopted statewide "massive resistance" programs. Many of the programs were founded on the pre-Civil War theories of nullification-interposition, i.e., that a "sovereign" state had the legal right to nullify a Federal decision within its borders if the state found the decision unacceptable. The Civil War supposedly buried the theory.

All these "massive resistance" programs attempted to use the façade of a legal framework to thwart desegregation. Some programs allowed local school districts to close the public schools in order to avoid a Federal court integration order. However, only in Virginia, in Prince Edward County, was this tactic successfully used. A Federal district court in 1962 ordered Prince Edward County to reopen the schools, but county authorities refused to comply with the order and appropriated no funds to operate a public school system in 1963–1964.[7]

[6] *Aaron v. Cooper*, 358 U.S. 1 (1958).
[7] *Allen v. Prince Edward County School Board*, 207 F. Supp. 349 (1962).

Certain states, including Virginia, have also provided a tuition system which would allow the state to award tuition grants to students to be used in private segregated schools. Georgia has such a law, but in 1963 the Georgia Legislature reduced the funds in the tuition grant appropriation bill and several urban counties have withdrawn from the program. At least in the urban centers of the South there is sufficient organized support in favor of a quality public school system so that efforts to close public schools and use an inferior and privately operated segregated system will probably be unsuccessful. Help Our Public Education (HOPE), a citizens' group in Georgia lobbied in the early 1960s against the Georgia school-closing law. In 1961 the Georgia Legislature followed Governor Vandiver's recommendation and repealed the school-closing laws and substituted tuition grants and a pupil placement law.

Pupil placement laws. All the states of the Confederate South adopted state pupil placement or assignment laws sometime after May, 1954. These laws direct either a state or local board to enroll and assign pupils individually to schools. The criteria for assignment—orderly and efficient administration of the school, effective instruction, the pupil's standards, the pupil's academic preparation and scholastic ability—have no surface relationship to race. When these laws were first challenged in 1958 they were upheld because on their face they contain no impermissible standard.[8] However, subsequent litigation has demonstrated that where these laws are used race is a principal factor in administration of pupil assignments.[9] The truth of the matter is that pupil placement laws are a none too subtle means of providing for token integration. As the Circuit Court of Appeals for the Fifth Circuit said in 1962:

> This court . . . condemns the Pupil Placement Act when, with a fanfare of trumpets, it is hailed as an instrument for carrying out a desegregation plan while all the time the entire public knows that in fact it is being used to maintain segregation by allowing a little token integration.[10]

Atlanta used the pupil placement law to satisfy a Federal court order for integration of eleventh and twelfth grades in the fall of 1961. By

[8] *Shuttlesworth v. Birmingham Board of Education,* 162 F. Supp. 372; affirmed, 358 U.S. 101.
[9] For example, *Green v. School Board of Roanoke,* 304 F.2d 118 (1962).
[10] *Bush v. Orleans Parish School Board,* 308 F.2d 491 (1962).

the spring of 1962, 118 Negro students were attending previously all-white schools. The Atlanta school board approved 86 Negro applications in June, 1963, to transfer to predominately white schools in September, 1963. While it is true that the only public school integration achieved in Georgia by the spring of 1963 was in Atlanta, still the Atlanta program is a prime example of tokenism. Atlanta, like other Southern cities, assigns Negro children to the most convenient Negro school and white children to the most convenient white school. The placement laws operate only upon the application of a particular Negro or white student for transfer.

Rezoning and transfers. School attendance zones based on pupil residence and the capacity of the school is one of the oldest methods used in public education for apportioning pupils among schools. On its face a school attendance zone law is not unconstitutional. However, the transfer system has been administered in the South so as to avoid integration once a school district has been forced by court order to desegregate. For example, under the Nashville plan a pupil is entitled to receive a transfer from the school in which rezoning places him, if he finds himself assigned to a school that previously served the other race or to a school or class in which members of the other race are in a majority. In the first four years of the plan's operation in Nashville, all white children assigned to formerly Negro schools or schools predominately Negro requested and received transfers, thus leaving the schools with a totally Negro enrollment. In 1963 the Supreme Court declared the Knoxville and Davidson County, Tennessee, laws unconstitutional. Both of these transfer plans were almost identical to the Nashville plan. The Court again reiterated that race is not a permissible standard in public education. While the lower Federal court had declared that the plan was not an evasive scheme for segregation, the Supreme Court characterized the plan as a one-way ticket to continued segregation.[11]

The neighborhood school: Segregation by housing. A court order requiring desegregation in the Albany schools would probably not result in integration. Discriminatory housing practices and low economic status have confined most of the Albany Negroes to the Harlem district. In the event of a desegregation order this residential pattern would be used to perpetuate segregation by means of the neighborhood school system. Such a method of racial segregation is not unique

---

[11] *Goss v. Board of Education of Knoxville*, 83 Sup. Ct. 1405 (1963).

to the South. Segregated school systems in the North and West, particularly in urban elementary schools, are maintained by the neighborhood school plan.

On September 3, 1962, a group of Northern Protestant, Catholic, and Jewish representatives were arrested for partricipating in the Albany demonstrations. When Police Chief Pritchett ordered their arrest he remarked to them "Go back to your homes. Clear your own cities of sin and lawlessness." Probably the average Northern reaction to this was that it was just one more childish Southern attempt to ignore the crucial issue of segregation in the South. In part, this is a legitimate reaction. Segregation is certainly more serious in the South than elsewhere in the nation; more serious because it is more pervasive and because it is perpetuated by the help of the law. Yet the North is beginning to awaken to the seriousness of its own racial segregation problem in public education. There is growing recognition in the North and West that school boards have over the years consciously and sometimes unconsciously gerrymandered neighborhood school zones to conform to residential racial patterns.[12]

The first Northern desegregation decision in public education involved a public school in New Rochelle, New York.[13] In the New Rochelle case the Federal district court found that the school board had intentionally created a racially segregated elementary school and the board was required to implement a court-approved integration plan.

The New Rochelle situation is illustrative of several problems in desegregation. The school board attempted to resolve the problem by allowing any child to transfer out of the all-Negro elementary school to any other elementary school in the city. This free transfer approach was immediately criticized by those who feared that an influx of Negroes into previously all-white schools would have serious educational consequences for both white and Negro students. However, after one year of operation, little if any harm was done to the educational progress of white children. The Negro children in New Rochelle came from lower socioeconomic groups, and they have less measured educational aptitude than the white children. In their new schools they generally performed in the lower quarter of their classes.

[12] United States Commission on Civil Rights, *Civil Rights U.S.A.: Public Schools North and West, 1962*, Government Printing Office, 1962, p. 1.
[13] *Taylor v. Board of Education*, 191 F. Supp. 181 (1961).

But the performance of white children did not suffer and some Negro children showed a dramatic improvement in their performance. Moreover, discipline problems for some Negro children decreased.

SCHOOL SEGREGATION: THE CONTINUING IMPASSE Twelve years after the *Brown* decision racial segregation in public education continues on a national scale. While a limited amount of progress has been made in the South, particularly since the passage of the 1964 Civil Rights Act, *de facto* school segregation has actually increased in the North and West in the past decade. This increase in school segregation is the result of the continuing exodus of whites with school age children from the central cities to the suburbs. By 1966, with only limited data available, nine major cities in the East and Midwest had Negro majorities in their school system. Indeed, in Washington, D.C., the first segregated school system to desegregate, over 90 per cent of the public school population is Negro. Title VI of the Civil Rights Act of 1964 authorizes Federal agencies to withhold funds from federally assisted programs which practice racial segregation. While most school districts submitted statements to the U.S. Office of Education indicating compliance with Title VI, the fact remains that no funds were withheld during the 1965–1966 school year and segregation continued.

In 1966 the U.S. Office of Education released a report, "Equality of Educational Opportunity." The report was based on a 1965 national sample of 4,000 public schools. It revealed that almost 80 per cent of all white pupils in the first grade attended schools that were from 90 to 100 per cent white and that over 65 per cent of all Negro pupils in the first grade attended schools that were between 90 and 100 per cent Negro. Although the report found that the home background of a pupil has more effect on his educational achievement than the quality of the school he attends, it also found that a Negro pupil's level of achievement was helped more by high quality schools than that of a white pupil. The report pointed out that by tangible standards Negro schools are inferior to white schools. In Negro primary classes the average class size was 32 whereas it was 29 in white primary classes. Physical facilities were also inferior. For example laboratories for chemistry and physics courses were less likely to be found in predominantly Negro schools than in white schools.

In 1966 Harold Howe II, United States Commissioner of Education, stated that desegregation had been a failure. If by this he meant that we have failed to achieve a substantial degree of racial integration in the public schools, it would be difficult to disagree. It is doubtful, however, whether the Supreme Court's decision in the *Brown* case was intended in 1954 to achieve this goal. It seems likely that what the Court intended in 1954 was the destruction of the more obvious features of the legal framework which supported racial segregation. To a large extent that framework has been destroyed. What the Court and the nation at large did not realize in 1954 was that the Negro would not be contented with mere legal equality. During the first decade after the *Brown* decision the civil rights movement did focus on the removal of legal barriers to racial justice, particularly in education. Yet the removal of these barriers did not result in desegregation. Thus racial segregation is no longer, if it ever was, a strictly legal issue. Racially segregated communities, the greatest single barrier to desegregation in the schools, are a political issue and politics must provide the forum for solutions.

RACE DISCRIMINATION AND VOTING

The right of citizens of the United States to vote shall not be denied or abridged by the United States or by any State on account of race, color, or previous condition of servitude.

The Fifteenth Amendment, March 30, 1870

We are a little fed up with this voter registration business. . . . We want our colored people to live like they've been living for the last hundred years— peaceful and happy. . . . You know, Cap . . . there's nothing like fear to keep the niggers in line.

A Georgia sheriff, Summer, 1962

The Constitution of the United States is the supreme law of the land except in the Terrell counties, and there another law prevails. "Terrible Terrell" is a Black Belt county adjacent to Dougherty County. Approximately two-thirds of the residents of Terrell County are Negroes. If life with dignity is a difficult matter for the Albany Negro, for the Terrell County Negro it is close to impossible.

After the first Reconstruction and the withdrawal of Federal troops in 1877, the Negro was systematically disenfranchised throughout the South by a variety of methods—the poll tax, literacy tests, the white primary, and force and fear. However, from the early part of the twentieth century down through the 1940s, the Supreme Court was generally hostile to Southern attempts to discriminate against the Negro's right to vote. The Court struck down the use of "grandfather" clauses in literacy test requirements in 1915.[14] Grandfather clauses were statutory provisions which exempted one from a literacy test if he could vote in 1866 or if he were the lineal descendant of one entitled to vote in 1866 or anytime prior to 1866. When the South turned to the white primary as a means of excluding the Negro from political power the Court also declared it unconstitutional.[15] By 1947 there were 645,000 registered Negro voters in the 12 Southern states. By the end of 1960 there were 1,361,944 registered nonwhite voters in these states out of a nonwhite voting-age population of 5,131,042. Part of this relatively low Negro registration can be attributed to sheer voter indifference. But racial discrimination in Negro suffrage continues to be a major reason.

Voting is the one area in civil rights where the Federal government has extended its power to help the Negro. The leadership came originally from the Supreme Court in the white primary cases. Then, in 1957, 1960, 1964, and 1965, Congress passed the first civil rights legislation in eighty years. The legislation focused on protecting voting rights. The 1957 act allows the Attorney General to institute civil suits in Federal district courts to prevent and redress racial and other arbitrary interferences with the right to vote.[16] This places the burden on the Department of Justice and not on the individual Negro. Under the 1960 act, the Federal district courts are authorized to appoint voting referees after finding a pattern or practice of discrimination.

The first suit under the 1957 act was filed in Terrell County. The Federal district court held the congressional legislation unconstitutional, and on appeal the Supreme Court reversed the lower court.[17] An injunction was then issued in 1960 against the Terrell County registrars. The following findings of the Federal district court in the Terrell County case are representative of the pattern of Southern voting discrimination:

1. The use of differently colored registration application forms for white and Negro voters

14 *Guinn v. United States*, 238 U.S. 347 (1915).
15 *Smith v. Allwright*, 312 U.S. 649 (1944).
16 42 U.S.C. § 1971 (1957).
17 *United States v. Raines*, 362 U.S. 17 (1960).

2. The keeping of separate registration and voting records for whites and Negroes

3. Delaying action upon registration applications of Negroes, but not of whites

4. Requiring a higher standard of literacy for Negroes than for whites when administering the literacy tests.[18]

In the Terrell County case several of the Negro applicants were college graduates and at least two held master's degrees; six were teachers. They all failed the literacy test! Without racial discrimination, literacy tests can be justified as a requirement for voters. Nineteen states, including a few Northern and Western states, have literacy requirements. While the Supreme Court has upheld literacy tests,[19] it has also declared that arbitrary literacy laws are in conflict with the Fifteenth Amendment. In 1965 it ruled against the Louisiana literacy test, holding it a trap, not a test, ". . . sufficient to stop even the most brilliant man on his way to the voting booth." [20]

While the Terrell County officials were enjoined from racial discrimination in voter registration there has been no significant increase in Negro registration. Out of a white population of 4,533 there were 2,894 registered voters in 1960. Out of a Negro population of 8,209 there were 51 registered voters. By 1963 there were still less than 100 registered Negro voters in Terrell County. In Albany, however, out of 15,000 registered voters, approximately 5,000 were Negroes. The explanation for this disparity between Terrell and Dougherty counties is fear, intimidation, and the threat of economic reprisals. In the summer of 1962 rural Negro churches in Terrell County which were being used in the voter registration drive were burned. At one meeting Sheriff Mathews entered the church with several white men and questioned the Negroes and took down names. Mathews was subsequently indicted by a Federal court in August, 1962, for intimidation of Negro voters. A deputy marshal in Terrell was tried in January, 1963, on a similar charge by a Federal jury, which, after deliberating twenty minutes, acquitted the defendant.

In contrast to Terrell, the voter-registration drive in Albany has made a significant increase in Negro registration and foreshadows political power. Between July 1, 1962, and May, 1963, approximately

[18] *United States v. Raines,* 189 F. Supp. 121 (1960).
[19] *Lassiter v. Northampton County Board of Elections,* 360 U.S. 45 (1959).
[20] *Louisiana v. United States,* 380 U.S. 145 (1965).

one thousand new Negro voters were registered. In the fall of 1962 for the first time in Albany history a Negro ran as a candidate for the city commission. Although he was defeated, his candidacy did result in a runoff election. In the spring of 1963 Albany Negroes contributed to the defeat of bonds for the building of new police and county and city administration buildings. Leaders of the Albany Movement were arrested when they passed out antibond handbills. Prior to the 1962 fall elections Albany Negroes were required to vote in segregated polling places, and separate voting lists were maintained. In early 1962 a Federal district court held this unconstitutional; [21] in the fall elections the county abolished racially segregated polling places but did require a separate polling place for men and women. In October, 1963, Slater King, a leader in the Albany Movement, ran for mayor. He was defeated, but he placed second out of three candidates. Both of the other candidates were white. In Atlanta in 1962 Negroes were able to elect the first Negro state senator since the end of the first Reconstruction. Negro voting influence in Atlanta, Albany, and other Georgia urban areas also accounted for the election in 1962 of Governor George Sanders, a moderate segregationist, who was opposed by an ardent segregationist. Total Negro registration in Georgia in 1962 was approximately two hundred thousand. Negroes constitute 25.4 per cent of the voting-age population in Georgia, but only one-third of the eligible Negroes are registered.[22]

BLACK BELT COUNTIES In a study conducted by the United States Commission on Civil Rights of 17 Black Belt Southern counties, 97 per cent of the voting-age Negroes were not registered. Why does such a large segment of the population refrain from registering and voting? The explanation for the disparity in Negro registration between an Atlanta or an Albany and a Terrell County was concisely stated by the former mayor of Dawson in Terrell County when he said, "This is a feudalistic society." And it might have been added that the Negroes are the serfs, only today they are called sharecroppers or tenants.

Cotton continues to be the major crop in the majority of Black Belt counties. Few of the Negroes own their own land. They are sharecroppers or tenants and are caught in a one-crop economy. The system retains many of the evils of the old plantation-slave system.

[21] *Anderson v. Courson*, 203 F. Supp. 806 (1962).
[22] See United States Commission on Civil Rights, *Voting*, Government Printing Office, 1961.

The Negro is dependent on white landowners, gin operators, and store owners. Financial indebtedness to the whites is something he lives with his entire life. His family income and education are well below those of the whites, and he lives in overcrowded and unsound houses. It is difficult enough for the average white family in these counties; their education and income are usually well below the national and state averages. But for the Negro, life is even more appalling. Consigned to poverty and economic dependence, the Negro in Black Belt counties spends his life in total isolation from political power. "The Negro, even in counties determined to treat him fairly, would rather not risk having his tax assessment increased or lose his credit, by attempting to register to vote." [23] The President of the United States might as well be the man in the moon as far as the Black Belt Negro is concerned. What is important to him is who is the county sheriff. The President of the United States will become important to him only when the President helps him to replace any sheriff who regards Negroes as serfs. As in the field of education, the solution is not simple. One thing, however, is certain—Federal court decisions alone have little efficacy in a Black Belt county. When it became obvious that the 1957 and 1960 legislation was insufficient to remedy the problem, Congress again passed voting rights legislation. In 1963 Congress proposed the Twenty-Fourth Amendment. The Amendment was adopted by the states in January of 1964. It prohibits a poll tax in Federal elections. Subsequently the Supreme Court declared poll taxes unconstitutional in state and local elections.[24]

In 1964 Congress made it illegal to administer registration and voting laws in a discriminatory manner. In particular the 1964 legislation addressed itself to the problem of the unfair administration of state literacy tests. Again the legislation was found to be inadequate and in the 1965 Voting Rights Act the problem of literacy tests was attacked. The 1965 legislation allows the Attorney General to institute litigation to enforce the guarantees of the Fifteenth Amendment and in such suits Federal courts may suspend state literacy tests if they conclude they are used to deny persons the right to vote on account of race or color. The legislation further provides for Federal courts to authorize the appointment of temporary Federal examiners to serve in place of state and local registration officials. By the end of 1965,

[23] United States Commission on Civil Rights, *The Fifty States Report*, Government Printing Office, 1961, p. 104.
[24] *Harper v. Virginia Board of Elections*, 86 Sup. Ct. 1079 (1966).

Federal examiners were designated for 32 counties in Alabama, Mississippi, Louisiana, and South Carolina.

The 1965 legislation proved to be more effective in ending racial discrimination in voting rights [25] than previous legislation. In the five Deep South states Negro registration increased 33 per cent in the first eight months of the new legislation. However, fear of white reprisals continues to keep down Negro registration in Southern states. The ambush of James Meredith during the 1966 Mississippi March on Fear lends support to this position. Nonetheless Negro political strength is on the rise in the South and Negro votes are beginning to influence the power structure. In the spring of 1966 the incumbent sheriff of Dallas County, Alabama, site of the famous Selma March, was defeated for renomination by a moderate with the help of Negro votes.

PUBLIC FACILITIES

Shortly after the Birmingham sit-in demonstrations in the spring of 1963, President Kennedy was reported to have said, "The right to buy a cup of coffee is only enjoyed by a man with a dime." The implication of this was obvious; the Negro must first gain economic power before he will be accepted at a white lunch counter. A similar argument was made by a famous Georgia Negro. Booker T. Washington said in his Atlanta Exposition speech, "The opportunity to earn a dollar in a factory just now is worth infinitely more than the opportunity to spend a dollar in an opera house." Washington's advice was given in 1895.

There is certainly strong evidence to support the contention that the degree of private and public racial discrimination is closely related to the economic power of the Negro. In Terrell County the median family income for Negroes is $1,313; in Albany it is $2,430, and in Atlanta, $3,108. But in each instance the median family income for Negroes is half or less than half of the median for white families. Negroes have rejected the advice of Booker T. Washington. They have concluded that discrimination in employment cannot be separated from discrimination on a bus or at a lunch counter. Securing economic rights is inexorably tied to being accepted at a lunch counter.

From the beginning, leaders of the Albany Movement have worked for desegregation of public facilities. To accomplish this goal they have used both direct action and legal action. With the assistance

[25] See United States Commission on Civil Rights, *The Voting Rights Act: The First Months*, Government Printing Office, 1965.

of the Student Non-Violent Coordinating Committee they were able to force the bus terminal to comply with the ICC regulation on desegregation. However, in January, 1962, a young Negro girl was ordered to the rear of an Albany city bus. A boycott of the Albany bus line began; by March, 1962, bus company operations had ceased. When operations were resumed they were on an integrated basis with white and Negro drivers.

During the winter months of 1962 the Movement began sit-in demonstrations at white lunch counters and an economic boycott of white downtown stores. In the first quarter of 1963, Albany was the only major Georgia city to report a decrease in sales tax receipts. Throughout the summer and fall the sit-ins and demonstrations continued at lunch counters, at the downtown white library, and at white parks and swimming pools. The city maintained a branch library for Negroes in the Harlem district and also a Negro park and pool. The city officials responded with mass arrests. When this did not have the intended effect, the city was granted a temporary injunction against demonstrations in the Federal district court. When the injunction was overturned on July 23 by the United States court of appeals, the city closed the main library, the Lee Street branch library, and all municipal parks and pools ". . . in the interest of public safety."

The leaders of the Albany Movement then sought to enjoin racial segregation in various Albany public facilities and to have the city segregation ordinance declared unconstitutional, but their requests were denied by Federal District Judge Elliott.[26] The city commission also declared the public recreational facilities surplus property and repealed all segregation ordinances. The main library was reopened in March, 1963, with "vertical" integration, but the city has accepted bids for the sale of the recreational facilities to private parties. In June, 1963, the publisher of the local daily newspaper purchased the Tift Park pool and tennis courts for $72,000. He immediately announced that these facilities would reopen and operate on a white basis. The court of appeals refused to issue an injunction to prohibit the sale.

PUBLIC FACILITIES AND THE FOURTEENTH AMENDMENT There is no question that racial segregation in a facility operated or leased by a state, city, or county is a denial of equal protection of the laws. There is also little doubt that such segregation is still widely

[26] *Anderson v. Kelly*, 32 F.R.D. 355 (1963).

practiced in the South. Immediately after the *Brown* decision, the Supreme Court handed down summary decisions declaring the Montgomery city segregation ordinance invalid and ordering the desegregation of city parks, beaches, and golf courses in New Orleans, Baltimore, and Atlanta.

The South ignored the full meaning of these cases. In public facilities as in public education, the South has generally not acted except upon court order. The *Atlanta* case involved the golf courses [27] and was decided in 1955. But Atlanta city swimming pools were not integrated until the summer of 1962 and then by a Federal court order. Nonetheless, while Atlanta was peacefully integrating a dozen pools in 1962, Albany was closing its pools and making plans to sell them in order to avert integration.

In 1963 the Supreme Court took note of the delay in desegregation in public facilities. In denying the pleas of the city of Memphis for further delay in the integration of public parks and recreational facilities the Court observed:

> We cannot ignore the passage of a substantial period of time since the original declaration of the manifest unconstitutionality of racial practices such as are here challenged, the repeated and numerous decisions giving notice of such illegality, and the intervening opportunities heretofore available to attain equality of treatment. . . . Brown never contemplated that the concept "deliberate speed" would countenance indefinite delay in elimination of racial barriers in schools, let alone other public facilities not involving the same physical problems or comparable conditions.[28]

SIT-INS AND TRESPASS When the tempo of Negro resistance to segregated public facilities increased in the late 1950s, the Supreme Court had to face a new issue in the civil rights battle. Negro movements throughout the South were increasingly turning to direct action to complement the previously favored legal approach of seeking injunctions. In 1961 and 1962 the Supreme Court required lower Federal courts to enjoin racial discrimination in private eating facilities operated in government buildings in Wilmington, Delaware, and Memphis, Ten-

[27] *Holmes v. City of Atlanta*, 350 U.S. 879 (1955).
[28] *Watson v. City of Memphis*, 83 Sup. Ct. 1314 (1963).

nessee. However, in 1961 the Court handed down its first "sit-in" or direct-action case. The case involved a sit-in by Negro students in 1960 at a white lunch counter in a Kress department store in East Baton Rouge, Louisiana. The students were ordered to leave by the police and when they refused they were arrested for disturbing the peace, even though they were following the usual sit-in practice of maintaining silence and perfect decorum. The Supreme Court reversed the Louisiana convictions for lack of evidence to support a finding that such conduct could validly disturb the public peace.[29] Again in 1966 the Court reversed state sit-in convictions, this time in a public library sit-in case. In the 1966 case the narrowly divided Court observed that the First and Fourteenth Amendments ". . . embrace appropriate types of action which certainly include the right in a peaceable and orderly manner to protest by silent and reproachful presence, in a place where the protestant has every right to be, the unconstitutional segregation of public facilities." [30]

Sit-ins in private businesses raise a somewhat different legal problem from segregation in a government facility. The equal protection of the laws clause of the Fourteenth Amendment prohibits state racial discrimination, but the amendment does not apply directly to private discrimination. The crucial issue in the sit-ins is whether private discrimination is not indeed state discrimination when the police and the laws are used to enforce it.

In two 1963 decisions the Court again overturned sit-in convictions. In a South Carolina case, *Peterson v. City of Greenville*,[31] the trespass convictions of Negro boys and girls for peaceful sit-ins at a Kress store were voided as well as the local segregation ordinance, which required segregated lunch counters. In Albany the city officials took comfort in the *Peterson* decision, because in March, 1963, they repealed all city segregation laws, seemingly making racial segregation a private matter. Again, it was another game of legal charades.

However, on the same day as the *Peterson* case, the Court also voided trespass convictions in peaceful sit-ins where there was no local ordinance requiring segregation. In this New Orleans case the Court held that segregated service at private restaurants was being maintained by an order of the police chief to prohibit Negroes from seeking desegregated service in private restaurants. The Court pointed out that

---

[29] *Garner v. Louisiana*, 368 U.S. 157 (1961).
[30] *Brown v. Louisiana*, 86 Sup. Ct. 719 (1966).
[31] *Peterson v. City of Greenville*, 83 Sup. Ct. 119 (1963).

the state may not achieve segregation in private restaurants by ordinance, as in the *Peterson* case, or ". . . by an official command which has at least as much coercive effect as an ordinance." [32]

The question still to be decided is whether, in the absence of overt evidence of a state or local governmental segregation policy, Negroes may be arrested by police and convicted on trespass charges solely because of their race. In other words, may privately inspired segregation be assisted by the local police and judiciary through arrests and convictions for trespass? While the Court avoided this issue, in 1948 the Court did hold that race restrictive covenants, while not illegal, nonetheless might not be enforced in the courts. To do so would make the state a party to racial discrimination in violation of the equal protection clause.[33]

Justice Douglas, in a concurring opinion in the New Orleans case, remarked:

> When the doors of a business are open to the public, they must be open to all regardless of race if *apartheid* is not to become engrained in our public places. It cannot by reason of the Equal Protection Clause become so engrained with the aid of state courts, state legislatures, or state police.

THE 1964 CIVIL RIGHTS ACT   Following the Birmingham riots of 1963 President Kennedy proposed Federal legislation to ban racial discrimination in most public accommodations as a burden on interstate commerce. Governor Wallace of Alabama termed the proposals "the involuntary servitude bill." Wallace said, "The free and uncontrolled use of private property is the basic and historic concept of Anglo-Saxon jurisprudence." There is no absolute right to the uncontrolled use of private property in the English common law nor has such a proposition ever been accepted in the United States. As Chief Justice Holt remarked in 1701 in *Lane v. Cotton:*

> Wherever any subject takes upon himself a public trust for the benefit of the rest of his fellow-subjects, he is *eo ipso* bound to serve the subject in all the things that are within the reach and comprehension of such an office, under pain of an

[32] *Lombard v. Louisiana*, 83 Sup. Ct. 1122 (1963).
[33] *Shelley v. Kraemer*, 334 U.S. 1 (1948).

action against him. . . . If on the road a shoe fall off my horse, and I come to a smith to have one put on, and the smith refuse to do it, an action will lie against him, because he has made a profession of a trade which is for the public good, and has thereby exposed and vested an interest of himself in all the King's subjects that will employ him in the way of his trade. If an innkeeper refuse to entertain a guest where his house is not full, an action will lie against him. . . .[34]

The United States Supreme Court expressed the same proposition in 1877. Chief Justice Waite, speaking for the Court, said:

When one becomes a member of society he necessarily parts with some rights or privileges which, as an individual not affected by his relations to others, he might retain. . . . Looking then to the common law . . . we find that when private property is "affected with a public interest, it ceases to be *juris privat* only." This was said by Lord Chief Justice Hale more than two hundred years ago . . . and has been accepted without objection as an essential element in the law of property since. Property does become clothed with a public interest when used in a manner to make it of public consequence, and affect the community at large. When, therefore, one devotes his property to a use in which the public has an interest, he, in effect, grants to the public an interest in that use and must submit to be controlled by the public for the common good. . . .[35]

The question is not whether drugstores or department stores are places of public business with public consequences—that they are is an acknowledged proposition of the law. The question rather is whether there is a serious social consequence resulting from the racial discrimination practiced by these public businesses.

President Kennedy's recommendation became Federal law when Congress passed the 1964 Civil Rights Act. Title II of the act prohibits

[34] 88 Eng. Rep. 1458 (1701).
[35] *Munn v. Illinois*, 94 U.S. 113 (1877).

Housing Agency. War housing was segregated, but Negroes did receive about 15 per cent of all the units. However, in the privately financed wartime-priority housing the Negroes received only 4.3 per cent.

After World War II, the FHA and the newly created VA took some hesitant steps toward an "open occupancy" policy. The FHA dropped its restrictive covenant policy and modified the language of the "Underwriting Manual." Nevertheless the FHA continued its policy of allowing builders and lenders free choice as to who could buy or rent FHA-insured houses. In effect, the change meant little more than that the Federal agencies no longer had a declared policy of racial discrimination in housing.

THE HOUSING ACT OF 1949: UNFULFILLED PROMISE   In 1949 Congress passed a major housing act which stated an overall national housing goal. Congress declared that national policy was "the realization as soon as feasible of the goal of a decent home and a suitable living environment for every American family." That goal is increasingly being realized for white Americans. But for the overwhelming majority of Negroes, Mexican-Americans, and Puerto Ricans it has remained an empty promise. While the VA and FHA no longer guarantee loans on property with racial restrictive covenants this has not produced equal housing opportunities for minority groups. Furthermore, both the FHA and the VA have cooperative agreements with some states that have antidiscrimination housing laws. In theory they will insure no loans in these states for discriminatory builders and developers. In practice, neither agency had suspended a builder or developer by the end of 1962. By 1959 it was estimated that less than 2 per cent of the homes insured by FHA since 1946 had been available to minorities.[37] There is also strong evidence to support the conclusion that the VA has directly engaged in racial discrimination in the resale of reacquired VA-insured properties.

PUBLIC HOUSING AND URBAN RENEWAL   Not only have the policies of the major Federal loan-insurance agencies failed to end housing discrimination, but in public housing and urban renewal projects the Federal government has actually intensified residential segregation. Urban renewal frequently amounts to nothing other than "Negro clearance." Some middle-income Negroes have been able for the first time to get new housing under the FHA relocation programs which

[37] *Ibid.*, p. 63.

accompany urban renewal. For the bulk of the lower-income Negroes, however, urban renewal has actually diminished the total
housing available to them.

The public housing projects are intended to provide standard
shelter for low-income families. The projects are constructed and
operated by local governments under federally insured bonds and an-
nual Federal contributions to maintain the low-rent feature. Since the
end of World War II open occupancy policies in public housing projects have prevailed in 32 states. But even with open occupancy policies,
de facto segregation based on site selection has been the reality. In
those states where a separate but equal policy prevails, segregation
is governmentally maintained.

THE SUPREME COURT AND RACE DISCRIMINATION IN HOUSING   In the past,
racial discrimination in housing has not been subject to any considerable degree of judicial scrutiny. There is little doubt that many FHA
and VA and local housing policies have been inconsistent with the due
process clause of the Fifth Amendment, but most of the discriminatory
policies have been by subtle administrative determinations which are
difficult to identify and prove in a court.[38] The Supreme Court has
ruled that racial restrictive covenants, while not illegal, may not be
enforced in a state court. To do so would make the state a party to
discrimination in violation of the equal protection clause.[39] The Court
has also ruled that a city may not attempt to zone residential districts
into white and Negro sections.[40] But what cities have been unable to
accomplish by obvious means they have attempted to accomplish by
more subtle methods. In 1961 the United States Commission on Civil
Rights reported instances of the use of the power of eminent domain
to condemn housing projects in all-white communities. The housing
was being built either by Negroes or by a developer who intended to
sell it to Negroes. The incidents occurred in Oregon, California, Illinois,
and Missouri. In each incident the city discovered the land was
needed for some public purpose only after it became public knowledge that Negroes would be residents of the new homes. The evidence
in each case was strongly presumptive that the local governments were
motivated by race prejudice.[41]

[38] Charles Abrams, *Forbidden Neighbors,* Harper & Row, Publishers, Incorporated, New York, 1955, p. 304.
[39] *Shelley v. Kraemer,* 334 U.S. 1 (1948).
[40] *Buchanan v. Worly,* 245 U.S. 60 (1917).
[41] United States Commission on Civil Rights, *Housing, op. cit.,* pp. 132–137.

TABLE 1 UNEMPLOYMENT RATE BY COLOR, 1948-1965

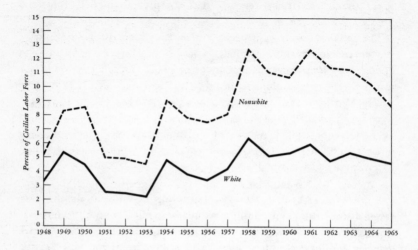

SOURCE: U.S. Department of Labor, *The Negroes in the United States*, Bulletin no. 1511, June, 1966, Government Printing Office, 1966.

TABLE 2 MEDIAN INCOME OF FAMILIES, 1964

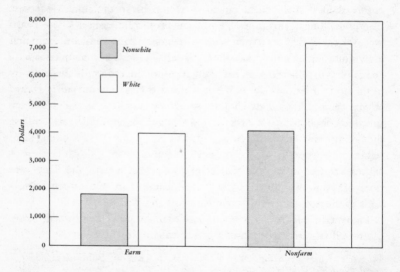

SOURCE: U.S. Department of Labor, *The Negroes in the United States*, Bulletin no. 1511, June, 1966, Government Printing Office, 1966.

"THE STROKE OF THE PEN"   In 1960 Senator Kennedy campaigned on a claim that only a "stroke of the pen" by the President was needed to end discrimination in housing. After his election, President Kennedy waited eighteen months before signing Executive Order no. 11063. The November 24, 1962, "equal opportunity in housing" order does not bind the entire housing field. The order does not cover homes financed under so-called "conventional mortgages," that is, financed without guarantees under the VA or FHA programs. The order does prohibit racial discrimination in all *future* housing aided by Federal loans, contribution, insurance guarantees. It is estimated that the order will cover 50 per cent of suburban housing and 25 per cent of housing in all areas. The order established an Equal Opportunity in Housing Committee to coordinate the implementation of the new policy by the Federal agencies. However, there were months of delay after the order was signed before the committee was fully established, and no budgetary requests were made in 1963 to provide the committee or the affected agencies with the necessary manpower to implement the new policy.

By the middle of the 1960s urban ghettos were still increasing and Negroes were being denied a choice in an open and competitive housing market. When President Johnson proposed a national fair housing law in 1966 his proposal met with sharp criticism from the National Association of Real Estate Boards and a cool congressional response. The 1966 Johnson proposal banned racial discrimination in all housing. As passed by the House of Representatives the measure exempted individual homeowners, boarding houses, and owner occupied apartments of four units or less. Thus the measure covered only large apartments and new housing which constitute approximately 40 per cent of the nation's housing. Due to the opposition of Senate Minority Leader Dirksen the 1966 Civil Rights Act died in the Senate and with it the housing title.

"BLACK POWER"   The Watts riots of 1965, the Chicago and Cleveland riots of 1966, and the cry of "black power" in 1966 were indications of the deepening gulf between white and black America.

The urban Negro lives in an environment of rising expectations. Migration from the rural South to the urban North was to be the fulfillment of a promise of a decent life. The promise has not been satisfied. His economic position improves when he migrates to the North, but the gap between Negro and white income is still great. In 1964, 37 per cent of Negro families had incomes below $3,000.

This compares with only 15 per cent of white families at the same income level. In the South 50 per cent of Negro families had incomes below $3,000 as compared with 25 per cent of such families in the West and North. Table 1 illustrates the persistent gap between white and nonwhite unemployment rates. Table 2 illustrates this income gap for farm and nonfarm families during 1964.

The policy of gradualism and moderation which has characterized much of the leadership of the NAACP, the Urban League, and the Southern Christian Leadership Conference, is being challenged by the "black power" slogan of CORE and SNCC. The slogan undoubtedly reflects the growing disenchantment of younger Negroes with a white alliance which has failed to narrow the gap between black and white America. Roy Wilkins and Martin Luther King both rejected the "black power" slogan of Stokely Carmichael because of its disturbing connotations of black racism and black violence. The important thing about the slogan, however, is not that it could be used by racial bigots, but rather that it signals a coming to the foreground of younger Negro leaders who feel that the broad masses of Negroes must play a larger role in the Negro movement.

Review Questions

1. What was the separate but equal doctrine?

2. What is the general argument that supports greater governmental restraints on public business establishments which do solicit general public patronage than on businesses which do not solicit such patronage?

3. Is there any evidence of public or private race discrimination in your community? If so, how is it manifested?

4. In what manner did the FHA contribute to racial discrimination?

5. What are the disadvantages of judicial desegregation in public education?

6. What judicial precedent is there against the state lending its coercive power to assist private racial discrimination?

FREEDOM OF THE PRESS: CENSORSHIP AND OBSCENITY

Chapter 2

In the early months of 1961, an American publishing house announced the publication of Henry Miller's *Tropic of Cancer*. The book had been originally published in Paris in 1934, but in the United States it had been effectively banned as obscene and had only circulated *sub rosa*. Miller's work is an autobiographical journal of a penniless American in Paris in the early thirties. It is a book which rages on about sex and self-expression and in the process travels the "full length" in sex fantasy. But neither sex nor Miller's elephantine humor can relieve the tedium of the book. It is a journal of total night, without love or compassion. It is also an embarrassing book because twenty-seven years after its initial publication it has become the dated novel of a self-conscious bohemian. In spite of this, the American publication of Miller's *Tropic of Cancer* was a minor milestone in the changing moral climate.

As recently as 1950, *Tropic of Cancer* had been denied admission into the United States. In slightly over ten years a copy might be found in the corner drugstore, that is, in most corner drugstores. When Grove Press published over 2,500,000 copies, it appeared as if the sales would be amazing. The Federal restraints on the book had been lifted. The Post Office and the Customs Bureau dropped their cases against *Tropic of Cancer*. However, state and local law-enforcement agencies were quick to move against the book under their own obscenity laws. By the end of 1962, *Tropic of Cancer* had become the subject of over 50 criminal cases, and over 600,000 paperback copies had been returned to the publisher by distributors.

The *Tropic of Cancer* issue is illustrative of a delicate problem faced by the law and society: how can freedom of press be reconciled with obscenity? Obscenity does matter. It is of special importance when it presses upon the young and immature, when it twists and distorts sex and marriage. Yet for all this, the scales weigh heavily in favor of a skeptical view of censorship. History cannot tell us how to reconcile the current issue, but it can offer evidence which should lead to a cautious attitude when we hear the cause of censorship of obscenity advocated.

CENSORSHIP IN HISTORY

Censorship by governmental authority can be traced back to Greek and Roman societies and on into early church history. Early censorship by church and state was directed primarily at heresy and political attacks on the state rather than obscenity. The phenomenon of widespread censorship of obscenity was a product of modern technology and its consequent mass culture. Modern technology began with Caxton's introduction of the printing press in England in 1476. The next two centuries witnessed a growing concern about the problem of public morals and obscene books. Still, the principal concern of both church and state was over the influence that an uncontrolled press might have in politics and theology.

Defense of a free press. While political and religious censorship continued intermittently throughout the sixteenth and seventeenth centuries there was a growing opposition to governmental interference with the press. The best-known and most widely quoted defense of a free press was made by John Milton in his *Areopagitica* in 1644, and practical arguments offered against censorship today are largely the same arguments that Milton presented over three hundred years ago. Now, as then, the argument begins with the assumption that man is a free creature with the ability to make reasonable choices. Free men must have the right to seek the truth. They must have "the liberty to know, to utter, and to argue freely according to conscience. . . ."

Perhaps the greatest appeal today for Milton's treatise is his practical defense of the freedom to read. Milton posed the question which the defenders of a free press have asked in all subsequent generations:

> How shall the licensers themselves be confided in, unless we can confer upon them, or they assume to themselves above all others in the land, the grace of infallibility and uncorruptedness?

More recent critics of censorship were less charitable when they noted that the case for censorship must stand or fall on its being administered by the wisest man in the world:

> But no wise man would accept such a post. As things are constituted it is pretty safe to assume that any given censor is a fool. The very fact that he is a censor indicates that.[1]

Puritanism.   For many years a favorite theme of critics of censorship has been that the healthy attitude toward sex which had existed in literature was suddenly changed by a group of sour-faced Puritans bent upon making everybody as miserable as possible. There is some truth and a considerable amount of fiction in such a proposition. The dour and self-righteous Puritan that people think of today is largely the product of the cartoonists. It is true that the Puritans were concerned with a reformation in manners; they did tend to emphasize piety and chastity; and they did expect man's life to be directed to the glory of God. They were not opposed to pleasure and certainly not opposed to sex. About all that can be legitimately ascribed to Puritans in this area is an influence on later legal developments. But they be-

[1] Heywood Broun and Margaret Leach, *Anthony Comstock: Roundsman of the Lord*, Literary Guild, New York, 1927, p. 275.

queathed a heritage of squeamishness of speech and action upon which the neo-Calvinists in the eighteenth century embellished and enlarged.

The Restoration. Few periods in literary history have been totally free of earthy literature. Chaucer wrote "The Miller's Tale" and Shakespeare is still known to many as the bawdy bard. Of course, Chaucer also wrote romances for knightly circles and Shakespeare is also remembered as the Biblical bard. Still, some periods appear to have been freer in sex expression in literature than others. The Restoration was such a period.

Hippolyte Taine said, with quaint bluntness, that when we pass from the noble portraits of Van Dyck in the reign of Charles I to the figures of Peter Lely in the reign of Charles II we have left a palace and lighted on a bagnio.[2] Much of Restoration verse and drama stands out as sensual and bawdy. It seems that the Earl of Rochester set out to bury heroic love and came close to doing just that with his bawdy verses. The foes of contemporary sex censorship delight in informing their readers that the present censorship of obscenity is really a ridiculous denial of the earthy robustness of our literary history, particularly as it is exemplified by the Restoration period. Certainly Restoration drama does afford abundant opportunity to stress the acceptance of sex as a legitimate tool in literary style. But the fact remains that what is termed erotic realism today is not some unbroken heritage of the past. Dryden and Rochester abound in erotica but this simply reflects a basic aristocratic cynicism in morals and manners, a reaction to the interlude of the Puritans, rather than an acceptance of obscenity. Finally, the uninhibited works of the court wits were not written for mass audiences but rather for the aristocracy, a fact which most opponents of obscenity censorship ignore.

The eighteenth century. It was not until the eighteenth century that a literary reading public emerged in England and the American Colonies. Two seemingly contradictory developments occurred concurrently with the emergence of this new reading public: an increasing sensitiveness on the part of the government to the circulation of allegedly obscene printed matter, and a general acceptance of the broad principle of freedom of the press.

It is not surprising that with the increased circulation of the press there was also an increase in the volume of obscene books and a resultant concern over their distribution. A Scottish minister wrote in the first quarter of the eighteenth century that:

[2] Hippolyte Taine, *History of English Literature*, 2d ed., Edmonston and Douglas, Edinburgh, 1872, vol. I, p. 458.

> . . . all the villanous profane and obscene books
> and playes printed at London by Curle and other are
> gote doun from London by Allan Ramsey, and lent
> out, for an easy price, to young boyes, servant
> weemen of the better sort and gentlement, and vice
> and obscenity dreadfully propagated.[3]

What the minister was witnessing was the rise of the lending or circulating library. This institution was made possible in the early eighteenth century by the availability of cheap paper and a rising urban population. Gradually the governing class became alarmed over the social problems which they expected to result from this new freedom in reading. Curl, the lending librarian spoken of by the Scottish minister, was in fact the first person convicted in an English secular court for publishing an obscene book. The title of the book was *Venus in the Cloister or the Nun in Her Smock*. The case which was decided in 1727, marked a fundamental change in English law.[4] Only a few years before the *Curl* case the courts had refused to accept jurisdiction in a similar case.[5] After the *Curl* case it was accepted that obscene publications could be restrained.

Nonetheless freedom of the press was gradually accepted as a principle of American and English government at the same time that government censorship of obscenity was occurring with increased regularity. The most celebrated American case was tried in New York in 1734. Peter Zenger was arrested on a charge of seditious libel, accused of printing a political attack on the governor. At that time in England and in the Colonies seditious libel was not defined by any law, and hence a man did not know in advance whether his publications would offend those in authority or not. The heart of the matter was that while the defendant was tried before a jury, the jury was not allowed to decide whether in fact the book or paper was libelous. In the *Zenger* case the court ruled that the defense could not introduce evidence to prove the truth of Zenger's statements and further that the court, and not the jury, would determine whether the statements were libelous. The jury refused to convict Zenger. The result of this case was that the people had asserted a new authority over the government's attempt to control the press.

Throughout the remainder of the eighteenth century the principle

---

[3] Robert Wodrow, *Analecta: Or Materials for a History of Remarkable Providences, Edinburgh Printing Company, Edinburgh*, 1843, vol. III, p. 515.

[4] *Rex v. Curl*, 2 Stra. 788 (1727).

[5] *Queen v. Read*, 11 Mod. 142 (1708).

of freedom of the press gained further acceptance. In 1776 the Virginia Bill of Rights was adopted and it included a statement that the "freedom of the press is one of the great bulwarks of liberty, and can never be restrained but by despotick governments." When the Federal Bill of Rights was adopted in 1791, it included a restriction in the First Amendment against the Federal abridgment of a free press: "Congress shall make no law . . . abridging the freedom . . . of the press."

While freedom of the press was gaining recognition as an operating principle of government, few believed that the principle was absolute. There was general acceptance of the rule that the government was precluded from prior restraint, that is, prepublication censorship of the press. The great eighteenth-century legal commentator, Sir William Blackstone, wrote:

> The liberty of the press is indeed essential to the nature of a free state; but this consists in laying no previous restraints upon publications, and not in freedom from censure for criminal matter when published.

Thus, while the law of libel was considerably narrowed in the late eighteenth century, it has remained a legitimate means of punishing the malicious defamation of a person by publications. Similarly, the publication of obscenity was not considered immune from governmental restraint.

THE VICTORIAN CONSCIENCE

With the advent of the Industrial Revolution, first in England and later in the United States, literary taste underwent a vast transformation. Sometime in the late eighteenth century the novel became dainty, and sex was all but banished from the reading public.

The prelude to what we today call the Victorian conscience started in the 1780s with the evangelical movement. The rising middle class had more leisure time for reading and the evangelicals set about substituting "good" reading matter for "bad." A new moral orthodoxy was introduced. Novels had to have a moral purpose and, more importantly, they had to be "proper" companions for women and children. As the drawing room became the center of the middle-class family, books had to be sufficiently decorous to lie on the drawing-room table without offending the eyes of a young lady. The book became a symbol of refinement and taste.[6]

In fairness to the evangelicals and the early Victorians, it must be said that they were reacting to new social and moral problems, problems which were the by-products of the Industrial Revolution and the urban movement. There was an increasing market for pornography—from the highly priced erotica designed for the bibliophiles to the vulgar trash designed for the mass public. In a limited way, then, the new conscience was a means of self-defense.

Unfortunately, the evangelicals and the early Victorians did not limit their goals to a mere self-defense against the flood of pornography. Inevitably their drive to purify literature carried with it a deep suspicion of all imaginative writing. The book became the potential snare of the devil. When Thomas Bowdler took the blue pencil to Shakespeare, he was but reflecting the era's morbid concern with human passions.

Victorian censorship. By the middle of the nineteenth century Victorian censorship was in full swing. In the 1850s book production became cheaper and the reading public increased again. The expected happened: editors began to press writers to treat sex in a gingerly fashion, or better still, not to treat it at all. Leslie Stephen, an editor, cautioned Thomas Hardy in the sixties to "remember the country parson's daughters. *I* have always to remember them." In 1853 the English Parliament passed the first act prohibiting the importation of pornography. The United States Congress had passed a similar statute in 1842. In 1857 Parliament passed the Campbell Act which empowered magistrates to order the destruction of obscene books and prints. This was followed in the United States by the passage in 1865 of the first postal law prohibiting the distribution of obscene printed matter in the mails. In the same year a Federal district court, acting under the 1842 customs law, prohibited the importation of shirt-front boxes embellished with a picture called "Susanna at the Bath" or "Diana and Her Nymphs." The government charged that the pictures were "too indelicate for family use."[7] All that remained to be done was to give a sweeping judicial definition to obscenity. The courts were quick to oblige.

The Hicklin test and "Comstockery" In 1868 Lord Cockburn

---

[6] See Amy Cruse, *The Englishman and His Books in the Early Nineteenth Century*, George G. Harrap & Co. Ltd., London, 1930.

[7] *Anonymous* No. 470, 1 Fed. Cas. 1024 (1865).

handed down his famous decision in the *Hicklin* case. The new definition of obscenity was:

> . . . whether the tendency of the matter charged as obscene is to deprave and corrupt those whose minds are open to such immoral influences and into whose hands a publication of this sort may fall.[8]

This meant that the starting point in the determination of obscenity was to be the moral level of a child. Furthermore, the court ruled that obscenity was not to be judged only by the tendency of the whole book, but also by isolated passages in the book.

In the United States the Hicklin standard was quickly adopted, and under the leadership of Anthony Comstock a noble army of fanatics set out to rid American society of obscenity. To Comstock, obscenity was the great trap for the young, for "it breeds lust. Lust defiles the body, debauches the imagination, corrupts the mind, deadens the will, destroys the memory, sears the conscience, hardens the heart and damns the soul." [9] Like his evangelical forefathers, Comstock let his zeal carry him to excesses. The result was a general distrust of imaginative literature.

Under Comstock's leadership the New York Society for the Suppression of Vice was founded in 1873. This was followed in 1874 by the founding of the Western Society for the Suppression of Vice, and in 1876, the New England Watch and Ward Society got under way in Boston. These societies, located in the principal publishing centers, were able to suppress books with the collaboration of the police. They became so powerful that they virtually dictated all the police arrests and even made citizens' arrests themselves. They suppressed everything from Whitman's *Leaves of Grass* and birth control literature to hard-core pornography. Comstock personally was able to boast that he had destroyed more than 50 tons of indecent books, 28,425 pounds of printing plates, and nearly 4 million obscene pictures!

It would be misleading to conclude from this that "Comstockery," a term introduced by G. B. Shaw, accounts for the romantic genteel tradition in American literature in the late nineteenth century. Comstockery was as much effect as it was cause. The genteel tradition was not the product of a single force but rather the product of movement and adjustment to the moral stresses of a rapidly in-

[8] *Queen v. Hicklin*, L.R. 3 Q.B. 360, 371 (1868).
[9] Quoted in Broun and Leach, *op. cit.*, p. 28.

dustrialized society. Alice Rice's *Mrs. Wiggs of the Cabbage Patch* and Anthony Hope's *The Prisoner of Zenda* were romantic escapes from the strains of the late Victorian era. Moreover, a great deal of Victorian censorship was cultural censorship privately imposed rather than public censorship. Indeed, with few exceptions the instincts of the literati were at one with those of the public in the sixties and seventies.

Transition from reticence to realism in literature. As the Victorian period stretched on into the nineties, a movement of protest against the genteel tradition arose. The family began to lose the place it had held under Victorianism, the drawing room and its reading habits were passing from existence, and a new generation of readers demanded the right to read what they liked—vice if they liked as well as virtue. Oscar Wilde said in his preface to *The Picture of Dorian Gray* in 1891, "Vice and virtue are to the artist material for his art. . . . There is no such thing as a moral or an immoral book. Books are well written or badly written." Authors on both sides of the Atlantic, Frank Norris, Theodore Dreiser, Thomas Hardy, G. B. Shaw, and James Joyce, broke away from the genteel tradition. They demanded the right to portray the bitterness and bleakness and not just the romance of their era. And this included a realistic or naturalistic approach to human passions.

The devotion of the new generation of authors to the rawness of human existence stirred the censors to new heights of activity. In retrospect it is strange that the censors were so enraged by the new realism. The early realism in Anglo-American letters was not sex sensationalism. On the contrary, it frequently had a curious look of moral temperance and purity. True, sex was restored to the novel, but in the hands of a Frank Norris or a Thomas Hardy the new heroines were never sexual *and* moral.

It mattered little to the Comstocks that many of the books they attacked in and out of the courts were indeed highly moralistic. What mattered to them was that human passions were being discussed for all the world, particularly the world of young ladies, to read about. Eventually the censors went too far. Federal customs officials banned the importation of such classics as Balzac's *Droll Stories*, the complete works of Rabelais, Boccaccio's *Decameron*, Ovid's *Art of Love*, and Aristophanes' *Lysistrata*. The Post Office even banned sex education materials and the police attempted to ban Shaw's *Mrs. Warren's Profession*. Shaw concluded that the excesses in censorship—Comstockery, as he called it—confirmed ". . . the deep-seated conviction of the Old World that America is a provincial place, a second-rate country-town civilization." [10] Comstock countered by calling Shaw an Irish smut peddler.

In part Shaw's criticism missed the point by a country mile. The standards Shaw was criticizing were as English as John Bull. The important point was that mid-Victorian moral standards were on the way out—in the family, in the theater, and in the courts. The English Hicklin test, so widely adopted in the United States, was too restrictive for the twentieth century, and it was shortly to be attacked.

The first major judicial assault on the Hicklin rule was made in 1913 in an opinion by Judge Learned Hand. The case was a mail obscenity action brought in a Federal district court against a book entitled *Hagar Revelly*. The novel is about the life of a young woman in New York who is compelled to earn her own living. She is represented as impulsive, sensuous, fond of pleasure, and restive under the monotony and squalor of her life. There is one unsuccessful and one successful seduction and finally a loveless marriage. Judge Hand upheld the Post Office ban on the book simply because the Hicklin test had been accepted by the lower Federal courts for over thirty years and he did not feel it proper at that date to disregard it. However, he did make this important observation:

> I hope it is not improper for me to say that the rule as laid down, however consonant it may be with mid-Victorian morals, does not seem to me to answer the understanding and morality of the present time, as conveyed by the words "obscene," "lewd," or "lascivious." I question whether in the end men will regard as obscene that which is honestly relevant to the adequate expression of innocent ideas. . . .[11]

In the year following Hand's decision, World War I began. This upheaval ended the already dying Victorian period. The full meaning of the change was not apparent for some time after the war, but the change could not be denied. American troops went to England and France, and the war was not all they were witness to. But before the

---

[10] Morris L. Ernst and William Seagle, *To the Pure*, The Viking Press, Inc., New York, 1929, p. 60.
[11] *United States v. Kennerly*, 209 Fed. 119, 121.

pendulum could swing too far in the direction of a commonsense approach to obscenity cases, the censors had to expose to the public and the courts just how far they intended to go in controlling the reading matter of the mature public. In 1929 a general censorship wave hit Boston, and when it was over, 68 books had been banned, including D.H. Lawrence's *Lady Chatterley's Lover*, Sherwood Anderson's *Dark Laughter*, Aldous Huxley's *Antic Hay*, Ernest Hemingway's *The Sun Also Rises*, and Theodore Dreiser's *An American Tragedy*. This was a grand finale to the twenties.

From reticence to realism in the law. By the early thirties it was apparent that some modifications would have to be made in the law of obscenity. In 1930 Congress amended the Tariff Act to allow the Secretary of the Treasury to permit the admission of the classics or books of recognized literary merit, regardless of their alleged obscenity. Three years later a Federal district court made the first successful attack on the Hicklin test.

In 1933 Judge John Woolsey in a United States district court in New York ruled that James Joyce's *Ulysses* was not obscene and lifted the ban on its importation. In lifting the ban Judge Woolsey attacked the main thesis of the Hicklin test: the isolated passages approach and the most susceptible person guide. He made the unprecedented move of reading the book himself. He found that there was a frankness in Joyce's approach, that portions of the book contained some dirty old Saxon words, and that the book as a whole did not have the leer of the sensualist. It was not "dirt for dirt's sake." On the contrary, he felt that the book was simply an honest attempt by means of a new literary method to describe the physical and mental life of the author's characters. While Judge Woolsey accepted a very broad definition of the word obscene—the tendency to stir sex impulses or to lead to sexually impure and lustful thoughts—he narrowed the application of the definition by conservative standards. First, he held that the court must consider the book as a whole and not isolated passages; and second, the book must be measured against its probable effect on a person with average sex instincts, against the normal person and not against the instincts of the perverted or the young.[12]

While the *Ulysses* case was an important breakthrough in the law of obscenity, it was only a lower Federal court case and as such it had to win adherents on the basis of its intrinsic soundness rather than on

[12] *United States v. One Book Ulysses*, 5 F. Supp. 182 and 72 F.2d 705 (1934)

the basis of its precedence in the judicial hierarchy. The censorship picture in the United States is necessarily complicated by the nature of the federal system. There are two separate judicial systems, state and Federal. The Federal government, as well as each state government, has its own obscenity laws. The picture is further complicated by the fact that, in addition to state statutes, many cities and counties have legislation governing obscenity. Thus there are literally hundreds of obscenity laws, each administered by separate law-enforcement agencies and interpreted by separate judicial systems. To the degree that uniformity is possible and desirable, it must come from the United States Supreme Court. After 1933 the *Ulysses* decision gained some recognition. However, the recognition was by no means uniform. For example, in 1945 Lillian Smith's *Strange Fruit* was banned in Massachusetts as obscene.[13] Three years later, in Pennsylvania, Erskine Caldwell's *God's Little Acre*, William Faulkner's *Sanctuary*, and James T. Farrell's *A World I Never Made* were cleared of obscenity charges.[14]

THE SUPREME COURT AND THE ROTH TEST

With the Federal courts in conflict, some following the Hicklin rule and some following the *Ulysses* case, and with the state courts in an equal muddle, it was apparent that the United States Supreme Court would have to face the constitutional issue of censorship of obscenity. Prior to 1957 the Supreme Court had never squarely faced the issue of the censorship of obscene printed matter. In that year the Court examined the validity of the Federal mail statute which declares obscene printed matter to be nonmailable.[15] The Court upheld the validity of the statute and declared that obscenity is not within the area of constitutionally protected speech and press. The Court noted that historically the constitutional protection for freedom of the press was not considered to cover every utterance. It reasoned that "all ideas having the slightest redeeming social importance—unorthodox ideas, controversial ideas, even ideas hateful to the prevailing climate of opinion—have the full protection of the guarantees. . . ." But the Court concluded that obscenity is utterly without redeeming social importance.

---

[13] *Commonwealth v. Isenstadt*, 318 Mass. 556 (1945).
[14] *Commonwealth v. Gordon*, 66 Pa.D.&C. 101 (1949).
[15] *Roth v. United States*, 354 U.S. 476 (1957).

The importance of the *Roth* case is not that it announced that obscenity is without constitutional protections; few people expected the Court to conclude otherwise. The importance of the case lies in its attempt to establish a standard for measuring what is and what is not obscene. The Court rejected the Hicklin test. Instead it cautioned that sex and obscenity are not synonymous. The portrayal of sex in art, literature, and scientific works is not itself sufficient reason to deny freedom of expression. On the other hand, "Obscene material is material which deals with sex in a manner appealing to prurient interest." In order that material which does not treat sex in such a manner may be protected, the Court established the following obscenity standard: whether to the average person, applying contemporary community standards, the dominant theme of the material taken as a whole appeals to prurient interest. Thus there are four vital parts to the *Roth* test: the material taken as a whole, the average person, contemporary community standards, and finally, the appeal to pruriency.

To the extent that the Court rejected the Hicklin test and substituted a more reasonable approach, the *Roth* case was certainly an improvement in the law of obscenity. However, the Court definition of obscenity in the *Roth* case left the law approximately where it was before—in a quandary. There is something circular in defining obscenity as that which appeals to a prurient interest, for prurient is defined as lascivious, and lascivious as obscene. Perhaps the case is best viewed not as a definition of obscenity, but rather as an attitude which can serve as a guide. The spirit of the case is that while obscenity may be the valid subject of *postpublication* criminal sanctions, nonetheless the judiciary must carefully guard against illegal infringements on free speech and press. "Ceaseless vigilance is the watchword to prevent their erosion by Congress or by the States."

Ceaseless vigilance: Post-Roth. While the Court has thus given positive sanction to the right of a state to control obscenity, other decisions after the *Roth* case have indicated a cautious attitude toward state controls. The court did uphold a New York statute which allows a limited injunction against the sale or distribution of printed matter found by trial to be obscene. Although such an injunction would issue prior to a judicial determination of the issue of obscenity, the Court stressed that there was no prior censorship involved since the law moved only after publication.[16]

During the same year as the *Roth* case the Court gave notice to the

16 *Kingsley Books v. Brown*, 354 U.S. 436 (1957).

states and to Federal agencies that they did not intend to open the floodgates to censorship. In four decisions without opinions the Court lifted the Chicago ban on the movie, "The Game of Love," and three postal bans on magazines, two nudist magazines, and one homosexual magazine.[17] The Court merely cited its decision in the *Roth* case as grounds for reversing the lower court decisions. Also, during the same term the Court struck down a Michigan statute which prohibited the sale of any obscene matter which might tend to incite minors to violent or depraved or immoral acts. The Court observed that to sustain such a law would be to burn the house to roast the pig. "The incidence of this enactment is to reduce the adult population to reading only what is fit for children." [18] The flaw was that the law prohibited the sale to anyone of matter tending to incite youth to immoral acts.

As further evidence of its cautious attitude toward the problem of censorship, the Court has informed the states that they may not adopt whatever procedures they please for dealing with obscenity. The freedom of a state to treat this problem must be limited by the constitutional protections ensuring freedom of expression and due process of law.[19] Thus a state may not authorize mass seizures of allegedly obscene materials without the protection of the Fourth Amendment. In a Missouri case the Court invalidated a mass seizure under warrants which did not specifically describe the particular obscene items to be seized.

The efforts of the police in the above case were directed against the so-called "girlie" magazines, magazines which have been under constant attack by the censors in recent years. The case is illustrative of the grave problems involved in any governmental program of censorship. Probably many people would be quite willing to sacrifice these magazines if they could be assured that in the process the government would not suppress materials entitled to free circulation. But not even the most qualified assurance can be given that local censorship programs will not invade constitutional freedoms. In the Missouri case the police seized 11,000 copies of 280 publications. Of these publications, 180 were found not to be obscene, but only after being suppressed for two months.[20]

[17] *Times Film v. Chicago*, 335 U.S. 35 (1957); *Mounce v. United States*, 355 U.S. 180 (1957); *Sunshine Book Co. v. Summerfield*, 355 U.S. 372 (1957); and *One, Inc. v. Olesen*, 355 U.S. 371 (1957).
[18] *Butler v. Michigan*, 352 U.S. 380 (1957).
[19] *Smith v. California*, 361 U.S. 147 (1959).
[20] *Marcus v. Search Warrants*, 367 U.S. 717 (1961).

Lady Chatterley and Mr. Summerfield. While the above cases of the Supreme Court are all important indications of a cautious approach to censorship of obscenity, the most important development after the *Roth* decision was not a Supreme Court case. In 1959 a Federal district court declared that the Postmaster General could not prohibit the mailing of D. H. Lawrence's *Lady Chatterley's Lover.*[21]

The *Lady* had been an obsession with censors in England and the United States since it first appeared in the late twenties and had been banned in both countries. When Grove Press published the first unexpurgated American edition it came up against one of the most aggressive censorship campaigns the Post Office had undertaken since the late twenties. Under the leadership of Postmaster General Arthur Summerfield and with the strong backing of congressional committees, the Post Office had declared war on the "smut peddlers."

Throughout the 1950s a variety of congressional committees had been accumulating testimony on the scope and structure of the national market in obscene materials. The Post Office Department estimated that there was a 500-million-dollar-a-year business in pornography. Most of the business was in slides and photographs of nudes. But the Department's campaign was by no means limited to stopping this business. It moved against girlie magazines, nudist publications, and other publications which it did not feel had a legitimate literary purpose. When the Federal courts refused to sustain the Department's ban on *Sunshine and Health* and on a homosexual publication, Mr. Summerfield was shocked. He observed in a speech before his Citizens' Advisory Committee on Literature that he could not conceive how certain items which he wanted the committee to examine could be "acceptable to our society today." Mr. Summerfield then presented each member of the committee with a copy of Lawrence's *Lady Chatterley's Lover.*

One of the most disturbing elements in the *Lady Chatterley* case was that postal officials not only considered themselves qualified to determine that *Lady Chatterley* was without legitimate literary purpose, but further, that such a determination was not subject to judicial challenge.

Judge van Pelt Bryan dismissed the Post Office's contention that its determinations were entitled to special weight and consideration. The Postmaster General had no special qualifications in literature which entitled his views to such special consideration. Furthermore, in hold-

21 *Grove Press v. Christenberry*, 175 F. Supp. 488 (1959).

ing the book not to be obscene, the judge warned that "it is essential to the maintenance of a free society that the severest restrictions be placed upon restraints which may tend to prevent the dissemination of ideas." [22]

By the early 1960s it seemed evident that the general tone of Supreme Court decisions was one of discouraging obscenity prosecutions. Yet the prosecutions on both the Federal and state levels continued and in 1966 the Supreme Court handed down three obscenity decisions, the net impact of which was to add confusion to its earlier decisions.

In the first decision a divided Court made a major modification in the *Roth* test. The decision opens the door to an increase in obscenity prosecutions. In a postal case the Court expanded the *Roth* test to include whether the publisher panders to the erotic interests of his customers.[23] In other words, a prosecutor may now include evidence of the publisher's pandering in the production, sale, and publicity of a given book. The Court acknowledged that this may well result in banning as obscene items which in another context would not be obscene. Thus the attempt in the *Roth* case to arrive at an objective standard is now undermined by a new relative concept.

The second decision expanded the "average" person aspect of the *Roth* test. In *Mishkin v. New York* the Court returned to the nineteenth century *Hicklin* test and sustained the conviction of one engaged in the publication and sale of books catering to sexual deviants. "Where the material is designed for and primarily disseminated to a group, rather than the public at large, the prurient appeals requirement of the *Roth* test is satisfied if the dominant theme of the material taken as a whole appeals to the prurient interest in sex of the members of the group." [24]

Both of the above cases would seem to indicate a return to a more conservative attitude. The third decision was, however, more in keeping with developments immediately after the *Roth* decision. In a decision involving the eighteenth century book *Fanny Hill* the Court reversed a judgment against the book because the state court had failed to consider that the book had some redeeming social value. The Court reaffirmed its position that in order for a book to be proscribed it had to be found *utterly* without redeeming social value.[25]

[22] *Grove Press v. Christenberry*, 175 F. Supp. 488, 502 (1959).
[23] *Ginzburg v. United States*, 86 Sup. Ct. 942 (1966).
[24] 85 Sup. Ct. 958 (1966).
[25] *A Book Named John Cleland's Memoirs of a Woman of Pleasure v. Massachusetts*, 86 Sup. Ct. 975 (1966).

MOTION PICTURES

Rape is a vicious and brutal act. To portray rape in a novel requires the skill of a master artist. To portray rape in a motion picture requires an even greater deftness. Ingmar Bergman did it in "The Virgin Spring." "The Virgin Spring" is adapted from a thirteenth-century ballad about the rape of a trusting young girl by two shepherds. It is a morality play about the good and evil in man. Critical to the setting is the twenty-four-second rape scene. Without the rape scene the enormity of the outrageous crime and the consequent inhuman action by the father is weakened. Unquestionably the rape scene serves an important artistic function. But the scene is also graphic, and graphic rape in a book or a motion picture is bound to stir the censor; it did in "The Virgin Spring." The Acadamy Award winner was denied a license in New York and in Texas until the rape scene was cut.

Censorship of motion pictures dates back to the pre-Hollywood days of the nickelodeon screens. Even before the silent-screen days of Vilma Banky or the later risqué films of Mae West, the censors had turned on the motion-picture industry. A few states adopted censorship boards and several cities established agencies for reviewing and licensing films. Industry was quick to respond.

Self-regulation. In a series of moves stretching over twenty-five years the industry approached self-regulation as an answer to the increasing pressures for governmental censorship. In 1909 the industry-supported National Board of Review was founded to preview films and improve the content of movies. In time the board was attacked as a tool of industry. In 1922 the industry formed the Motion Picture Producers and Distributors of America headed by a former Republican national chairman and Harding Cabinet member, Will Hays. The Hays Office was to preview scripts and films and award an industry seal of approval. However, risqué films continued and in 1930 the Hays Office adopted a tighter code containing numerous taboo subjects, such as sex perversion, childbirth, and illegal drug traffic. The major rule of the code was and is: "The sympathy of the audience shall never be thrown to the side of crime, wrong-doing, evil or sin."

But the Hays Office lacked effective powers of enforcement. Finally in 1934, under pressure from the National Legion of Decency, a Catholic group founded in 1933, the association gave the Hays Office the power to fine any member $25,000 for producing, exhibiting, or distributing any picture without the seal of approval. The new code was a tremendous success. It did what it was intended to do—it stopped the drive for governmental censorship.

The family picture. With the adoption of a new code in 1934, Hollywood embarked on a golden era. Talkies were now firmly established and the industry gained a vast middle-class audience. The "Family picture" was the vogue. The gangster movies of James Cagney gave way to the comedy of the Marx Brothers, the westerns, and the Shirley Temple films. It was the day of the happy ending.

The American film industry survived for the next fifteen years on pictures which met the approval of the Hays Office and the National Legion of Decency. However, by the late 1940s Hollywood faced a major economic threat—television. Television began to take away the big audiences for mediocre movies.

The adult picture. Hollywood's response to television and to increasing competition from foreign "art" films was the "adult" or mature picture. "A Streetcar Named Desire" appeared in 1952. "The Man with the Golden Arm" in 1954, and "Baby Doll" in 1956. These new films treated taboo subjects. In turn, they led to an attack within the industry on the priggish attitude of the Hays Office toward sex.

Unfortunately, the art or adult film brought in its wake a great deal of trash, American and foreign. Many of the new films were neither mature nor artistic but they were heavily larded with sex and passion. They reopened the question of governmental controls.

The courts and film censorship. Hollywood had survived through its major era, from the 1920s to the early 1950s, by self-regulation and an effective public relations campaign. Indeed, throughout the period it was, without any express constitutional protection, under freedom of press. In 1915 the Supreme Court had ruled that motion pictures were not protected by freedom of speech and press.[26] However, when self-policing began to break down and when film producers began to demand greater latitude it was inevitable that the Court would have to reexamine its 1915 decision.

In 1952 the Court reversed its earlier decision and held motion pictures within the protection of the First and Fourteenth Amendments. The case was based on the Italian film, "The Miracle." New York had denied it a license on the ground that it was sacrilegious. The Court noted that previous restraint was a form of infringement upon freedom of expression to be especially condemned and to be confined to

[26] *Mutual Film Corp. v. Industrial Commission,* 236 U.S. 230 (1915).

exceptional cases. That the film was branded as sacrilegious, with its connotations of religious orthodoxy, was not considered by the Court a valid exception. Nonetheless, the decision left the door open to exceptional cases where a governmental censorship might be upheld.

In less than two years after the 1952 decision, the Court struck down the censorship of the motion picture "M" by the state of Ohio and of "La Ronde" by New York.[27] Again, in 1959 the Court had a New York case before it. This time it was the film adaptation of the troublesome *Lady Chatterley's Lover*. New York had denied it a license because it "alluringly portrayed adultery as proper behavior under certain circumstances." The Court reversed the denial, observing that New York's action really amounted to censoring an idea.[28]

By 1960 the weight of opinion was against film censorship. Still the Court had never expressly denied the right of a state to adopt a licensing system and to require the editing of immoral or obscene films. In 1961 the Court, in a 5 to 4 decision, went against the weight of its former decisions and expressly stated that a properly drafted state censorship law would not violate constitutional protections.[29]

By 1965 four states—Kansas, Maryland, New York, and Virginia—and fifteen municipalities had film censorship boards. While the Court does not seem disposed to reverse its 1961 ruling, it has warned these boards that the burden of proving a film is unprotected rests with the censor and only a procedure requiring a prompt judicial determination suffices to impose a valid final restraint.[30]

Film classification. Some of the proponents of state controls have advocated a plan of film classification similar to the one used in England. Under this system the worst features of censorship, governmental editing and denial of license, would be substituted by governmental rating of films with the result that certain films would be closed to children. Classification plans were proposed in New York, New Jersey, and Missouri in 1963. Hollywood's reaction to the various plans has been largely negative. Some exhibitors and theater chains have adopted the practice of designating certain films as undesirable for children, but there is no industry-wide support for state classification. Hollywood wants the artistic latitude allowed to European producers, who operate under a classification system, but it does not want the consequent loss of markets.

---

27 *Superior Films v. Ohio*, 346 U.S. 587 (1954).
28 *Kingsley v. Regents*, 360 U.S. 684 (1959).
29 *Times Film v. Chicago*, 365 U.S. 43 (1961).
30 *Freedman v. Maryland*, 380 U.S. 51 (1965).

On the surface a governmental classification system holds out many promises, but such a system could force the industry back to the era of the "family picture," and in face of the appeal of television this would be the kiss of death to the industry. If governmental controls in this area are necessary they should be confined to the same controls which are allowable in literature, i.e., postpublication prosecution for the distribution and sale of hard-core pornography. True, motion pictures are more graphic than books, but so is television, and then where do we stop? We come back to the beginning, to Milton:

> How shall the licensers themselves be confided in, unless we can confer upon them, or they assume to themselves above all others in the land, the grace of infallibility and uncorruptedness?

Unresolved problems. The problems involved in the censorship of obscenity are far from solved. With the Federal courts gradually moving in the direction of limiting obscenity to hard-core pornography, the problem of definitions remains. The Supreme Court said in the *Roth* case that obscenity must be defined according to contemporary community standards. The unresolved problem is, what did the Court mean by community standards? Did the Court mean a national community or a state or a local community?

During the first five years of the Roth rule many of the lower Federal courts construed community to mean the local community, the community from which the jury is drawn, in which the judge and police officers live and work. Thus what is obscene to the average man in Dallas will not necessarily be obscene to the average man in Houston or New York City. The local approach has obvious limitations. It means that legitimate publishing houses which are engaged in national operations are required to anticipate hundreds of local standards in distributing magazines and books. The full implications of this approach is absurd. It means that a book which is entitled to full constitutional protections in one city can be held to be obscene in the next town. To openly acknowledge, in fact to invite, such a haphazard application of the law strikes at the very roots of justice.

Although the Supreme Court has not offered a complete solution to the problem, it has indicated that at least in postal cases the standard must be national. The Court reasoned that the postal statute is a national law and reaches all parts of the United States. By the same token, the Constitution is national. What is constitutionally protected in one part of the country should be protected in all the parts.[31]

It seems likely that if postal cases are to be judged under a national standard, then the two remaining Federal obscenity laws, the laws banning the importation of obscenity and its shipment in interstate commerce, must likewise be judged under a similar standard. Thus in national prosecutions we can eventually expect a national standard. It is difficult to predict whether the Court will attempt to require the state to adopt a national community standard in obscenity cases. From a logical point of view it would seem that the Court must do this. Since the constitutional protections ensuring freedom of speech and press apply with equal force to the states as well as to the Federal government,[32] it is unreasonable to allow the states to operate under a standard that is different from that which is required of the Federal courts when they are both applying the same constitutional law.

Freedom of the press, however, is not the only part of the Constitution. The federal structure is also a part of the Constitution and the existence of the federal system will weigh heavily against imposing a national standard on the states. It seems probable that judges and juries and police officers will continue to be influenced by prevailing local opinion. The trend in Supreme Court cases can be expected to instill in the courts a new spirit of tolerance for that which is personally distasteful.

Private and not-so-private censorship. Besides engendering a new spirit of tolerance in some areas, the attitude of the Supreme Court in obscenity cases has had other effects. The recent decisions have probably been a contributing factor in a rise in the number and scope of private censorship groups. The successors to the old vice societies have multiplied in recent years. There are now numerous national organizations engaged in active campaigns to stamp out obscene literature. The right of such groups to influence the public is, of course, basic to our free society. Indeed, in many respects it is easy to sympathize with these campaigns. Most of the organizations involved have as their principal purpose the protection of the youth of the nation from the crude and blatant sex sensationalism which is in such vogue today in popular literature. There is no question about the seriousness of the rise in juvenile delinquency. There seems to be little question either that the accelerated market in paperback books

[31] *Manual Enterprises v. Day*, 370 U.S. 478 (1962).
[32] See *Near v. Minnesota*, 283 U.S. 697 (1931).

has produced a rise in "blood and guts" sex novelettes. Paperbacks are cheap and easily accessible. Most of these novels of sex and violence are seriously lacking in artistic qualities. They are openly offensive to accepted standards of decency and they pander to the lowest tastes.[33] It would be comforting and easy to blame these books for the rise in juvenile delinquency.

There is little scientific support for the proposition that immoral books either cause or are a contributing factor to the delinquency of minors. The truth of the matter is that we do not know if there is any causal relationship between mass media and particular facts of antisocial behavior.[34] Assuming that books do have the kind of impact that the censors attribute to them, it does not follow that the proper solution to the problem is wholesale censorship. Mass campaigns to control immoral literature create at least as many problems as they solve.

In their sincere desire to protect the youth of the nation, many "citizens' committees" are all too quick to limit the reading matter of the adult population. It is undoubtedly true that American newsstands do contain material that is not suitable reading for a child. But the answer to the problem does not lie in wholesale removals of the materials from the market. The parental responsibility to supervise and educate a child should not be abdicated to a citizens' committee.

Additionally, the tactics of many of these groups leave a great deal to be desired. They frequently compile lists of objectionable books and magazines and then pressure law-enforcement agencies and distributors to accept their lists. Particularly distasteful is the practice of citizens' committees, self-appointed bodies, working in open concert with law-enforcement agencies to harass distributors. The usual pattern is for the committee to get the police to accept its list and then for the police to threaten distributors with prosecution if they do not withdraw the blacklisted materials. In Rhode Island a citizens' committee was established by state law. Entitled the Rhode Island Commission on Youth, the committee compiled lists of objectionable publications and circulated them to distributors. The lists generally

[33] See Margaret Dalziel, *Popular Fiction 100 Years Ago*, Cohen and West, London, 1957; Richard Hoggart, *The Uses of Literacy*, Chatto & Windus, Ltd., London, 1957.
[34] See Sheldon Glueck and Eleanor Glueck, *Delinquents in the Making*, Harper & Row, Publishers, Incorporated, New York, 1952; Marie Jahoda, "The Impact of Literature," a private paper circulated by the American Book Publishers Council, 1954.

contained girlie magazines, but some paperback books, such as Charles Mergendahl's *The Bramble Bush* and Grace Metalious's *Peyton Place* were included. In 1963 the United States Supreme Court held that this amounted to administrative prior censorship in violation of freedom of press.[35]

Another result of mass censorship campaigns is that they drive pornography underground, where it becomes the vocation of the least talented writers. Driving pornography underground gives it the status of a forbidden fruit and thus artificially creates a greater market for its production and distribution. In the history of the printing press and photography, there are few things that merit oblivion as much as girlie magazines. Censorship campaigns, instead of ridding society of the near obscene, of the cheap trash, help to sustain an interest in it. This does not mean that without legal sanctions obscenity in books or motion pictures would disappear. Some controls are an inevitable and indeed an essential part of contemporary society. Yet there is a vast difference between the quiet control of hard-core pornography by the government, the family, and the church, and the carefully contrived hysteria of a local censorship campaign. The state must continue to concern itself with hard-core pornography. It must devise methods for protecting the youth without limiting the mature public to a literary or film diet fit for a child, and it must do this without stifling the full and free expression of the creative artist. The state should leave to the home and the church the problem of treating borderline indecency. The state must have a bias for freedom.

Review Questions

1. What is the significance of the "book as a whole" test in obscenity cases?

2. What was the answer of the motion-picture industry to governmental censorship?

3. Is there any argument, however unsound, which could justify motion-picture censorship but not censorship of books?

4. What is the legal definition of obscenity?

[35] *Bantam Books v. Sullivan,* 83 Sup. Ct. 631 (1963).

5. Has your community recently witnessed any campaigns to censor obscenity in the bookstores, theaters, or newsstands? If so, who provided the leadership for the campaigns and to what extent did the government become involved?

THE LIMITS OF DISSENT: THE RADICAL RIGHT AND LEFT

Chapter 3

The scene, Madison Square Garden; the date, September 19, 1950; the occasion, the thirty-first anniversary of the American Communist Party; the speakers, Gus Hall, Elizabeth Gurley Flynn, and Benjamin Davis, Jr.:

> Hail the Soviet Union and its great leader Joseph Stalin, mighty and invincible.
>
> Wall Street and its filthy system of blood profit . . . have involved the United States in Korea.
>
> The pro-Fascist imperialists have brought forth [General Douglas MacArthur] because they need a man on a white horse to enslave the colored peoples of Asia, Africa and Latin America.[1]

---

[1] *The New York Times*, Sept. 20, 1950, p. 35.

The scene, a park in Washington, D.C.; the date, July 3, 1960; the theme, race hate; the speaker, the Commander of the American Nazi party, George Lincoln Rockwell:

> All right you dirty Jews, come on and holler. Come on you white people, get up front and move the Jews back. . . . Come on you bunch of Jews, let's hear it. . . . Yellow Jews. Communist Jews. Jew, Jew, Jew, Jew, Jews, Jews, sick-dirty Jews, filthy Jews. Dirty Jews. Rotten Jews. Miserable Jews. Shut up Jews. Go on and yell Jews.[2]

The average American finds the above statements disturbing and distasteful. He finds them distasteful because they have the ring of paranoia and disturbing because in their dogmatism they seem to threaten our pluralistic society. Yet America has an important stake in the George Lincoln Rockwells and the Gus Halls. The stake is not in their survival but in their freedom to survive. The very existence of democracy depends on the right to dissent and to dissent radically. For what is the meaning of freedom if it is merely the right to cheer the majority on?

But should America extend freedom of speech to the radical dissenters—dissenters, who, if they should ever achieve power, would forever end the right to dissent? Oliver Wendell Holmes, one of America's greatest jurists, gave two answers to the question: yes and no. No, said Holmes, freedom of speech is not an absolute, for:

> . . . the character of every act depends upon the circumstances in which it is done. The most stringent protection of free speech would not protect a man in falsely shouting fire in a theater, and causing a panic. . . . The question in every case is whether the words used are used in such circumstances and are of such a nature as to create a clear and present danger that they will bring about the substantive evils that Congress has a right to prevent.[3]

Eight months later Holmes said the creeds of such radicals should be heard because:

---

[2] *Rockwell v. District of Columbia,* 172 A.2d 549 (1961). Rockwell admitted saying only the last two lines.
[3] *Schenck v. United States,* 249 U.S. 47 (1919).

Persecution for the expression of opinions seems to me perfectly logical. If you have no doubt of your premises or your power and want a certain result with all your heart you naturally express your wishes in law and sweep away all opposition. . . . But when men have realized that time has upset many fighting faiths, they may come to believe even more than they believe the very foundations of their own conduct that the ultimate good desired is better reached by free trade in ideas,—that the best test of truth is the power of the thought to get itself accepted in the competition of the market.[4]

AMBIVALENT AMERICA

Holmes's ambivalence mirrors America in the twentieth century. As a democratic nation we have fought to preserve freedom throughout the world. We remained an open society in the 1930s when much of Europe and the Far East fell under the domination of totalitarian governments. In the period following World War II American aid helped nations preserve their independence from communistic totalitarianism. On the other hand, America has been often blind at home to the problems of political freedom. During World War I nearly one thousand persons were convicted of violations of Federal laws, which, among other things, made it a crime to utter or publish words intended to bring into contempt or disrepute the form of government of the United States.[5] These World War I convictions were largely directed not at German sympathizers but rather at the "radical" left's sympathy with the revolution that occurred in Russia during the war.

In World War II the Soviet Union was an ally of the United States and any sympathy that the radical left showed for the U.S.S.R. was indistinguishable from the general sympathy shown to the Soviet Union by its ally, the United States. In fact the only political free speech case which reached the Supreme Court during World War II involved the radical right, and the Court overturned the conviction.[6]

With the approach of the cold war in the late 1940s, America reverted to the Red scare atmosphere of 1920. The radical left was hunted down in government agencies, schools, labor unions, churches, universities, in Hollywood, and even in open cornfields. On September

[4] Dissenting in *Abrams v. United States*, 250 U.S. 616, 630 (1919).
[5] Sedition Act of 1918, 40 Stat. 553; repealed in 1921.
[6] *Hartzel v. United States*, 322 U.S. 680 (1944).

4, 1950, the Oklahoma City police arrested Alan Shaw, chairman of the Communist Party for Oklahoma and Arkansas, and four companions for disorderly conduct. The police found the group "huddled" around a laundry truck in an open field near the city limits. The police seized literature they described as "communistic." They justified the arrest because they thought the actions of the group might have led to a riot!

THE FEDERAL GOVERNMENT AND FREE DISCUSSION   With rare exceptions the Federal judiciary has followed the leadership of the Congress and the Executive in free speech and press cases.[7] In periods of internal crises, particularly when the crises are reflections of external threats, the judiciary has tipped the scales in favor of the exercise of state power as opposed to freedom of discussion. In part the law of free speech adapts to the fears and anxieties of the people. Yet the fears and anxieties of the people in times of stress are not infrequently irrational. Men feared witches and they burned women; men feared the Japanese and they imprisoned Japanese-Americans in "war relocation camps." Law in this sense is a cultural adaptation to the fears of the population based on the circumstances at any moment in time. When the circumstances change, the fears disappear and the legal system reverts to a position more consistent with the ideal of liberty.

It would be unfair to the judiciary to infer from this that the courts have acted solely on emotion or impulse. Even the most ardent democrats agree that there is a line to be drawn between liberty and license and that the line must shift in some degree from peace to war. Yet the judiciary is not absolved in war or cold war from distinguishing between legitimate questions of espionage and mere witch-hunts. Espionage is a reality but witches are the hallucinations of irrational men.

The Federal Constitution provides in Amendments One and Fourteen that neither the Federal government nor the state governments shall make any laws abridging freedom of speech and press. But from the time of the alien and sedition acts of 1798 through the Internal Security Act of 1950 the Congress has passed numerous laws restricting these rights. An occasional jurist like Justice Black has argued that when the First Amendment says that Congress shall make no law it means just that—Congress shall make no law. This absolutist position has never won wide judicial support. On the contrary, the majority

[7] See Harry N. Scheiber, *The Wilson Administration and Civil Liberties, 1917–1921,* Cornell University Press, Ithaca, N.Y., 1960; Herman Pritchett, *Civil Liberties and the Vinson Court,* The University of Chicago Press, Chicago, 1944.

position has been that when the framers of the Bill of Rights said Congress shall make no law abridging freedom of speech and press they recognized that certain areas of speech were outside the constitutional protection. In fact, while the Court has frequently struck down state laws in the area of speech and press, it was not until 1965, in *Lamont v. Postmaster General*, that the Court questioned the constitutionality of a Federal statute as conflicting with freedom of speech and press.

If one accepts a relativist position on freedom of speech, then the principal value of Holmes's doctrine of clear and present danger is that speech per se is not punishable. According to Holmes, the measure of a speech is the circumstances surrounding the speech. The stress is on the immediacy of the danger to good order and the public well-being. The doctrine attempted to balance individual rights against community rights. If there is no immediate danger to the community then there can be no governmental restriction.

The clear and present danger doctrine has had to compete with another tradition in the Supreme Court, a tradition which goes much further in limiting speech. This doctrine, variously called the "bad tendency" or "evil tendency" test, punishes evil speech per se, without regard to the immediate circumstances surrounding the speech. In two cases decided in 1920 the Court upheld convictions under the Espionage Act for making false statements about the United States with the intent to promote the success of its enemies. In sustaining the convictions the Court remarked of the statements that "their effect on the persons affected could not be shown, nor was it necessary. The tendency of the articles and their efficacy were enough for offense. . . ." [8] Five years later in the *Gitlow* case the Court again observed:

> The state cannot reasonably be required to measure the danger from every such utterance in the nice balance of a jeweler's scale. A single revolutionary spark may kindle a fire that, smoldering for a time, may burst into a sweeping and destructive conflagration.[9]

At least through the 1950s, it was apparent that the Congress and the Court were more inclined to follow the bad tendency test than the clear and present danger doctrine. In 1940 Congress passed the Smith

---

[8] *Schaffer v. United States*, 251 U.S. 466 (1920) and *Pierce v. United States*, 252 U.S. 239 (1920).
[9] 268 U.S. 652, 668 (1925).

Act. The statute proscribes certain kinds of speech and publication without regard to the weight of the circumstances surrounding the speech or publication. Under the act it is a criminal offense to willfully and knowingly conspire to teach and advocate the overthrow of the government by force and violence and to organize the Communist Party to that end.

In 1949, 11 leaders of the American Communist Party were convicted under the Smith Act. The convictions ultimately reached the Supreme Court, and while the Court claimed to be following Holmes, the decision was in the tradition of the *Gitlow* case. According to the doctrine adopted by the Court in the *Dennis* case an utterance may be deprived of its protection under the First Amendment when ". . . the gravity of the evil discounted by its improbability justified such invasion of free speech as is necessary to avoid the danger." [10]

It was not entirely clear from the *Dennis* case whether the Court intended to abandon any necessity for distinguishing between the advocacy of the abstractly evil doctrine of the violent overthrow of the government and the advocacy of action to accomplish the evil end. In 1957 in the *Yates* case the Court rejected any imputation that the mere advocacy of the abstract doctrine of violent overthrow of government was punishable under the Smith Act. The Court held that it is only the advocacy of action to accomplish the illegal overthrow that may be punished. The advocacy of the abstract doctrine, even though uttered with the hope of success, is too remote from concrete action to be regarded as criminal.[11]

The *Yates* case indicated a slight shift in America from the hysteria of the McCarthy period to a more relaxed atmosphere. While this has not resulted in any resurgence of the Communist Party in the United States it has meant that the Party can once again hope to gain access to public platforms. In fact the Party seems interested in creating a new image, an image which J. Edgar Hoover, Director of the FBI, feels is a false image of "legitimacy as a liberal political faction and freedom from foreign dictates." [12]

During the academic year 1961–1962 the Party embarked on a speaker's campaign in universities and colleges. From October, 1961, through June, 1962, Party leaders spoke before 48 college groups with an estimated audience of 43,000. In general they were more successful

[10] *Dennis v. United States*, 341 U.S. 494 (1951).
[11] *Yates v. United States,* 354 U.S. 298, 321 (1957).
[12] "Report of John Edgar Hoover, Director, Federal Bureau of Investigation, Fiscal Year 1962," Washington, D.C., 1962, p. 28.

in private schools than in state-supported institutions. They were denied permission to speak on numerous campuses, including Michigan State University, University of Buffalo, University of Washington, and Ohio State University. However, some universities refused to cancel Party speakers when organized pressures were directed against them. President Arthur S. Fleming of the University of Oregon upheld the right of Gus Hall, Party general secretary, to speak on campus. Fleming remarked:

> A University by its very nature cannot pay lip service to the concept of freedom of expression and then deny persons with whom it is in sharp disagreement the opportunity of giving expression to their views.

Governor Mark Hatfield of Oregon disagreed with President Fleming and declared, "I do not feel it is a question of free speech to deny a tax-supported program to one who advocates the overthrow of our government." The Americanism chairman of the Oregon American Legion seconded this view and noted:

> We have the utmost respect for the students' ability to differentiate clearly between the advantages of our way of life and the Godless ideology of Communism—when they are given the facts. They will not get the facts from Communist Gus. . . .

Naturally a university student might ask the Americanism chairman what special powers he has which allow him to see the truth.

The Americanism chairman shares with many other persons a deep conviction that communism as an organized movement does not follow the ground rules of democratic discussion, open and honest discussion, but rather has consistently argued in half-truth, distortions, and lies. Any examination of Communist Party literature in the United States in the past thirty years will support this view. Yet an assumption of a free society is that the people are capable of judging between fact and falsehood. In a free society, because it is free, there will be forces organized to expose falsehood.

COMMUNISM AND THE CONGRESS

To realize that communism is a conspiracy dealing in lies and distortions is one thing; to conclude from this that the best method of coping with it is to deny it the benefits of freedom is something quite

charge of Mrs. Knowles. The group asked for her discharge because it felt that "no security risk" should be employed in such a sensitive post as librarian.[15] As a result of this campaign, public funds were withdrawn from the library in 1955.

At this point the Fund for the Republic entered the controversy. The Fund was established in 1952 by the Ford Foundation to promote civil liberties. The directors of the Fund in 1955 included Paul Hoffman, formerly president of Studebaker Motor Company and first administrator of the European Recovery Plan—Marshall Plan; Chester Bowles, formerly head of the Office of Price Administration, former ambassador to India, former Governor of Connecticut; and Albert Linton, chairman of the Board of Provident Mutual Life Insurance Company. The Fund, through its president, Robert M. Hutchins, examined the Mary Knowles affair and in the early summer of 1955 decided to award the Plymouth Monthly Meeting $5,000 for its "courageous and effective defense of democratic principles." The award further divided the community and the Friends Meeting and ultimately led to additional congressional investigations.

In the late summer of 1955 the Senate Subcommittee on Internal Security summoned Mrs. Knowles to Washington, D.C. At the hearing Mrs. Knowles was asked again if she had ever been a member of the Communist Party or if she had ever known Herbert Philbrick. This time she refused to answer the questions not on the grounds of the Fifth Amendment but rather because she felt that the questions invaded her rights under the First Amendment and because the questions had no pertinency to national security. She freely testified that she was not presently a Communist or a member of the Communist Party and that ". . . for many, many years I have had no connection, direct or indirect with any organization on the Attorney General's list." She was subsequently cited for contempt of Congress, tried, and convicted. However, upon appeal the convictions were reversed. The court of appeals held that Mrs. Knowles had not been adequately informed of the subcommittee's purpose in questioning her or of the subject matter under investigation, or of the pertinency of any questions to a topic within the legal scope of the subcommittee's investigation.[16]

The House Committee on Un-American Activities conducted a hearing in the summer of 1956. The hearing was directed at the Fund for

[15] *The Plymouth Meeting Controversy,* Report of the Philadelphia Yearly Meeting of the Religious Society of Friends, Philadelphia, 1957.
[16] *Knowles v. United States,* 280 F.2d 696 (1960).

the Republic, and Mrs. Knowles was not a witness. The committee heard testimony from one employee of the Fund and from several members of the Friends library committee.

Shortly before the hearings were started the Fund had antagonized the House committee when it released a report about the evils of "blacklisting" of entertainers who had been accused of Communist leanings by witnesses before congressional committees. In June, 1956, one month before the hearings, Chairman Walters made a public statement in which he asked, "Is this foundation . . . a friend or a foe in our nation's death struggle against the communist conspiracy?"

When the hearings began in mid-July Chairman Walters prefaced the opening testimony with the remark:

> This committee wishes to know more about the factors which prompted the Fund for the Republic to consider the retention of a Communist, a defense of "democratic principles" worth $5,000 of its tax-exempt money?

The Fund accused Walters of a deliberate scheme to discredit it before the American public, and asked the committee to hear testimony from one of its directors. Walters assured the Fund that the committee would allow the Fund an opportunity to present its views. However, as the Fund undoubtedly suspected, Walters adjourned the hearing after one day without allowing it to present its story. Walters then announced:

> Our hearings on the $5,000 award made by the Fund for the Republic because of the retention of one who had been identified as a Communist further indicates the political subversion to which the Fund's tax-exempt money has been put.[17]

The story of Mary Knowles and the Fund for the Republic award is illustrative of the evils of congressional witch-hunting. Many honest and dedicated persons in Norwood and Plymouth Meeting were all too quick to pillory Mary Knowles not because she was a subversive, not because she was an incompetent librarian, but because someone had identified her as a one-time member of the Communist Party. Where is reason when Alerted Americans call for the firing of a village librarian as a "security risk"?

[17] *The New York Times*, Aug. 25, 1956, p. 12.

In these investigations, individual reputations were damaged, employment temporarily denied to Mrs. Knowles, the good name of a public-spirited organization blackened, the privacy of a religious body invaded, and its membership divided—and all to what purpose? It is obvious that the investigations were not undertaken with any expectation of uncovering new evidence which would be useful in drafting internal security legislation. The single purpose of all the investigations was to brand the Fund for the Republic and Mrs. Knowles as un-American, as subversives—and yet what a travesty on America's heritage of freedom! As Justice Black recently observed in a dissenting opinion in another congressional contempt case:

> . . . I believe that true Americanism is to be protected, not by committees that persecute unorthodox minorities, but by strict adherence to basic principles of freedom that are responsible for this Nation's greatness.[18]

The net result of twenty years of congressional investigations and prosecutions is that communism has all but passed outside the pale of critical discussion. To be sure, communism and the Communist Party were rejected in the United States long before the era of free-swinging congressional investigations and for far more substantial and valid reasons than were ever produced in a congressional investigation. Today internal communism has been reduced to a shadow and the Communist Party frequently appears to have about as many FBI informants as it does card-carrying members.

Unfortunately, in the process of attempting to protect internal security against the dangers of communism the militant anti-Communists, from congressional committees down to local "Americanism" committees, have spread confusion and suspicion. The left has become identified with communism in theory and with something approaching treason in practice. Few Americans will mourn the passing of revolutionary discussions about the violent overthrow of our government, but all should pause at the confusion between revolutionary communism and the left, and the resultant stifling of discussion of critical social and economic issues.

THE UNMOLESTED RIGHT

In sharp contrast to the radical left the radical right has suffered few deprivations of civil liberties. The radical right today enjoys a sub-

[18] *Wilkinson v. United States*, 365 U.S. 399, 422 (1961).

stantial audience in the United States; although it is not so cohesive as the old radical left, it has been successful in organizing a variety of militant groups, such as the Conservative Society of America, Project Alert, the Christian Crusade, the American Nazi party, and the John Birch Society. While many of these groups have been the subject of severe criticism there are no indications that governmental powers are being used, except in a few isolated instances, to suppress their views or restrict their rights of freedom of speech, press, and assembly.

The one radical right group which has come under repeated local governmental pressure is the American Nazi party. In 1960 the leader of the Nazi party, George Lincoln Rockwell, was convicted on two counts of disorderly conduct as a result of two public speeches he gave in Washington, D.C. In the first speech Rockwell asked the police to control the crowd and they refused. The police simply waited until the crowd broke through a roped enclosure and then arrested Rockwell. In both speeches Rockwell shouted anti-Semitic remarks in response to jeers and boos from the crowd. In the second speech, when the badgering from the audience grew intense, he ordered his men into the audience to surround the hecklers and shout them down. The Municipal Court of Appeals for the District of Columbia upheld the conviction, simply observing that freedom of speech is not absolute. The court was evidently most impressed with Rockwell's anti-Semitic responses to the hecklers, and one suspects that he was punished not for disorderly conduct but for his racial beliefs. The lower court relied on a 1942 Supreme Court decision which had sustained the conviction of a defendant who had called the city marshal "a God damned racketeer" and a "damned fascist." In that decision the Supreme Court noted:

> . . . such utterances are no essential part of any exposition of ideas and are of such slight social value as a step to truth that any benefit that may be derived from them is clearly outweighed by the social interest in order and morality.[19]

Some months after the Washington, D.C., incidents Rockwell applied for permission to hold a rally in New York City's Union Square to celebrate the birthday of Adolf Hitler. The permit was denied and

[19] *Chaplinsky v. New Hampshire*, 315 U.S. 568 (1942); cf. *Terminello v. City of Chicago*, 337 U.S. 1 (1940).

when Rockwell appealed the denial the New York court reversed the administrative decision. It was evident to the court that Rockwell's racial and political beliefs and the incidents in Washington, D.C., had been instrumental in the administrative denial. The court rightly pointed out that to make an inference ". . . that what he did yesterday he will do today," amounted to prior censorship.[20] Nonetheless when Rockwell reapplied for the permit to speak at Union Square it was again denied and he was offered an alternate site of a park on the waterfront.

In the year 1962 Rockwell experienced numerous difficulties with local audiences and local officials. He was booed off a platform in Lewisburg, Pennsylvania; barred from renting the Boston Arena; and forced to cancel a speech in Urbana, Illinois, for fear of violence; the Virginia Legislature revoked his organization's charter; and he was physically attacked by a student while making an address on the campus of San Diego State College. Being an American Nazi leader in 1962 had its limitations!

The only other recent incident affecting the right which compares with the denial of a public platform to Rockwell also occurred in New York City in 1962. William F. Buckley, Jr., the conservative editor of the *National Review* was refused permission to use the auditorium of Hunter College, a public institution. Since 1954 the *National Review* had leased the auditorium to sponsor lectures and the lease was canceled after Mr. Buckley introduced the French radical Jacques Soustelle at one of the lectures. In overturning the denial the New York court pointed out that since these public facilities were open to all there could be no prior censorship.[21]

The general picture on the radical right is that it is enjoying complete freedom from governmental restraint in organizing, soliciting funds, and propagating its views. For example, the John Birch Society, since its founding in 1958, has attracted sufficient strength to boast of congressional members, and articles from its journal *American Opinion* have frequently found their way into the *Congressional Record*. A former member of Congress, John Rousselot, became the Western states district governor for the organization after he was defeated for reelection in California in 1962. The group has freely organized cells in a number of states and its spokesmen appear as speakers before

[20] *Rockwell v. Morris*, 211 N.Y.S.2d 25 (1961).
[21] *Buckley v. Meng*, 230 N.Y.S.2d 924 (1962).

local service clubs, chambers of commerce, and patriotic societies.

So long as the radical right stays reasonably clear of any revolutionary dogma it is not likely to see its freedom of discussion suppressed by governmental authority. Most of the radical right groups are militantly anti-Communist, and in a cold war atmosphere their appeals will continue to strike a responsive chord in certain sectors of the American public. An appeal to God, country, and the free enterprise system is built-in insurance that what happened to the radical left immediately after World War II will not be the fate of the radical right.

While both the radical left and the radical right have strong antecedents in American history, they are, nonetheless, outside of the mainstream of American politics. It does not follow, however, that radical politics has never made and can never make contributions to American politics. Currently it is difficult to see what contributions could be expected from a group such as the American Nazi party, which so frequently appears as nothing more than a hate group, or the Communist Party, which is still the same blind follower of the Soviet Union that it was thirty years ago. But to silence the radical dissenters is to make a first step in the direction of political tyranny and cultural defeat. Each generation of Americans needs to be raised in an atmosphere where dissent is accepted as the right of free men. The Birchers and the Communists may have little to offer our government, but their freedom to dissent in the community is an important object lesson. The established order in law, in government, in science, in industry, and in the arts needs to be subject to challenge. If the right to challenge the government and the whole economic order is silenced, then the object lesson to the young becomes obvious: a premium is placed on silence and conformity.

Review Questions

1. According to Holmes, what determines the character of every action or speech?

2. State Holmes's argument for giving radicals the public platform.

3. What is the "evil tendency" test?

4. Do you consider the radical right a threat to the internal security of the United States government?

5. What is the Smith Act? The Internal Security Act?

6. What is the significance of the *Yates* decision?

RELIGION AND THE STATE IN THE POST-PROTESTANT ERA

Chapter 4

I believe in an America where the separation of church and state is absolute . . . where no church or church school is granted any public funds or political preference. . . . I believe in an America that is officially neither Catholic, Protestant nor Jewish . . . where no religious body seeks to impose its will directly or indirectly upon the general populace or the public acts of its officials and where religious liberty is so indivisible that an act against one church is treated as an act against all.

These words were given in an address in September, 1960, before the Greater Houston Ministerial Association. The speaker's implication was clear—"If elected President I will not build a secret tunnel to the Vatican." The words were those of Sen. John F. Kennedy. He had come to Texas as the Democratic candidate for President, but he came to the Greater Houston Ministerial Association, in the heartland of America's Bible belt, as a Catholic candidate. This was the last time a Catholic candidate for President will need to humble himself. The November, 1960, election of John Fitzgerald Kennedy marked the end of the Protestant consensus in national politics. This consensus had supported not only Protestant presidential candidates, but it had also sustained a pattern of church-state relations in which separation was balanced with cooperation and accommodation.

Some observers might conclude from such evidence as the nomination and election of John F. Kennedy that a new consensus in church-state relations is emerging and that it will be more favorable to the Catholic position than the consensus of the Protestant era. This might be consistent with the fact that Catholics in the United States are in a greater position of power now than at any previous time in American history. Furthermore, the passage of time will in all probability further enhance the power position of Catholics in America.

There may well be a new consensus emerging in the community which is more favorable to the Catholic position. But what has been occurring in the law, particularly in court decisions, is almost the opposite of this. Just at the time when Catholics were perhaps anticipating that their religious sentiments might receive the same degree of accommodation in the law and in the community that Protestant religious sentiments received in the past, the law has begun to move in another direction. The courts have been going in the direction of less cooperation and accommodation and more in the direction of neutrality in church-state relations.

This shift in the judicial position from cooperation to neutrality perhaps reflects a judicial insight into religion in America. It may be that the judiciary feels that any new consensus on the religious scene in America will never be so unified as the consensus of the Protestant era. Catholics are not the only group which has increased its power position in America. The past thirty years have also witnessed the rise of the American Jews. Furthermore, neither Protestantism nor atheism appears to be on the decline in America.

A less unified consensus could never support the degree of accommodation in the law which marked church-state relations in America for approximately 150 years. Viewed in this sense the trend toward neutrality need not be seen as a move from friendship to hostility, but simply as a recognition of the truly pluralist nature of the religious scene in America.

An unanswered question is whether the courts have not anticipated a greater breakdown in the old consensus than has occurred. That the old Protestant consensus appears to be on the way out is obvious in many urban areas, particularly in the Northeast and Middle West. But there is no truly national cultural trend in religion. The South, the rural Middle West, and the West are still overwhelmingly Protestant. What is evident in such a situation is the difficulty of reconciling sub-cultures to the law. It is nearly impossible for the Supreme Court not to expound "supreme" law. And yet, as we saw in the chapter on censorship, not every community is prepared to accept as "law" that which is seemingly antithetical to local culture.

CHURCH-STATE RELATIONS: THREE TRADITIONS

In the current controversy over church-state relations the key phrase is "absolute separation of church and state." Yet it is worth recalling that separation of church and state is not a phrase lifted out of the Constitution and it has only recently become a constitutional pillar. How absolute the separation should be is still an open question.

The colonial and Revolutionary periods in America produced three main traditions in church-state relations. They are the traditions of John Cotton, representative of the Puritan belief in an established church, of Roger Williams, the pious churchman who opposed estab-lishment, and of Thomas Jefferson, a deist and skeptic who advocated a wall of separation of church and state.

ESTABLISHMENT   Few of the colonial settlers came to America with any intention of rejecting the idea of an established church. While there was little colonial support for a theocracy there was general support in most of the Colonies for a state-supported church. John Cotton, one of Boston's great Puritan ministers, wrote in 1636:

> It is suitable to Gods all-sufficient wisdome and to the fulnes and perfection of Holy Scriptures, not only to prescribe perfect rules for the right order-ing of a private man's soule to everlasting blessed-

> ness with himselfe, but also for the right ordering
> of a man's family, yea of the commonwealth too,
> so farre as both of them are subordinate to spiritual
> ends.[1]

The core of the Puritan philosophy in church-state relations is contained in those few lines: the word of God is clear and explicit, the civil state must accommodate itself to the will of God, and the will of God requires all men to subordinate themselves to spiritual ends. What this meant in practice was an established church. At the close of the colonial period nine of the thirteen colonies had established churches. Yet establishment meant more than a state-supported church; it meant the close union of the church and state in social and religious endeavors.

Nonetheless there were other forces at work during the colonial period which weakened the Puritan position. The growing diversity of Protestant sects made the position of a Cotton impractical. Religious pluralism became an important factor in the movement away from the twins of establishment and religious toleration to disestablishment and religious liberty.

DISESTABLISHMENT Roger Williams of Rhode Island pointed in the direction of the future pattern of church-state relations in America when he wrote:

> All Civill States with their officers of justice in their
> respective constitutions and administrations are . . .
> essentially Civill, and therefore not Judges, Gover-
> nours or Defendeurs of the Spirituall or Christian
> State and Worship.[2]

Williams was a champion of religious liberty and disestablishment. While John Cotton saw the church and state as partners in the cause of God's truth, Roger Williams believed that spiritual truth was so rare that it should not be tied to the state. Rhode Island, under the leadership of Williams, and Pennsylvania and Delaware had no established churches. Williams maintained that all churches should exist on an equal footing and all individuals be allowed liberty of conscience.

[1] Perry Miller and Thomas Johnson, *The Puritans,* American Book Company, New York, 1938, p. 209.
[2] Quoted in Clinton Rossiter, *Seedtime of the Republic,* Harcourt, Brace & World, Inc., New York, 1953, p. 197.

By the end of the colonial period religious liberty for all Protestant sects was the accepted pattern. This shift from toleration to liberty carried with it a general loosening of church-state ties, but it had not resulted in any wholesale move for disestablishment. Disestablishment was a movement of the Revolutionary period. By the end of the Revolution a majority of the states had effectively abolished state churches. But final disestablishment did not come until 1833 in Massachusetts.

The Federal government, as distinct from the new state governments, began without an established church and when the Bill of Rights was adopted it contained a clause prohibiting Congress from enacting any law respecting an establishment of religion or prohibiting the free exercise of religion. But this limitation applied only to the national government until the 1930s then the Supreme Court interpreted the due process clause of the Fourteenth Amendment as embodying the same limitations on the states.[3]

While separation of church and state was largely accomplished in the states by the end of the eighteenth century, disestablishment did not mean complete separation. Many states, as yet unrestricted by any Federal limitation, continued well into the nineteenth century to actively cooperate with and aid various Protestant sects. Thus as late as 1852 New Hampshire retained in its constitution a permissive clause allowing local public support of Protestant religious instruction. Nor did religious liberty in the Revolutionary period and in the early years of the Republic mean full political rights for non-Protestants. Both Catholic and Jew suffered numerous civil limitations. The colonial settlers and their grandchildren had a deep suspicion of Catholics, and while freedom of worship was allowed, both Catholics and Jews were frequently disenfranchised and disqualified from public office by the states. New Jersey, North Carolina, and New Hampshire did not drop anti-Catholic political limitations until the middle of the nineteenth century.

SEPARATION Disestablishment began to take on the modern overtones of separation in Virginia in the late eighteenth century. Under the leadership of James Madison and Thomas Jefferson disestablishment began to mean a true severing of relations between church and state. While Roger Williams had approached separation out of a pious distrust of the state, Jefferson approached separation out of fear of

[3] *Hamilton v. Board of Regents*, 293 U.S. 245 (1934).

churches and an abiding skepticism of supernaturalism. It was Jefferson who coined the phrase a "wall of separation between church and state." In 1801 President Jefferson was requested by the Danbury Baptists Association to proclaim a day of fasting in connection with the nation's past ordeals. Both Washington and Adams had made similar proclamations. Jefferson refused and instead wrote the Danbury group:

> Believing with you that religion is a matter which lies solely between man and his God; that he owes account to none other for his faith or his worship; that the legislative powers of the Government reach actions only, and not opinions,—I contemplate with sovereign reverence that act of the whole American people which declared that their legislature should "make no law respecting an establishment of religion, or prohibiting the free exercise thereof," thus building a wall of separation between Church and State.[4]

By the middle of the twentieth century the no establishment clause of the First Amendment had all but been forgotten, and in its place Jefferson's phrase had been substituted, but with an absolutism which Jefferson had never intended. As an eighteenth-century deist Jefferson did not advocate absolute separation. For example, in the field of public education Jefferson was opposed to denominational control or influence, but he believed that the common core of religion should be included. In his draft of a statute to establish a public school system in Virginia, Jefferson merely held that there should be "no religious reading, instruction or exercise . . . inconsistent with the tenets of any religious sect or denomination."[5] Still, even Jefferson's nonabsolutist theory of separation was too advanced for his era. As long as Protestantism retained an overwhelming consensus in America, the Protestant churches and the states continued a lively partnership.

The Protestant crusade. When the Republic was established in 1789, the Catholic population numbered 35,000, with approximately 25 priests led by Bishop John Carroll. By 1822 the Catholic popula-

[4] Quoted in Anson P. Stokes, *Church and State in the United States,* Harper & Row, Publishers, Incorporated, New York, 1949, vol. II, p. 227.
[5] *The Writings of Thomas Jefferson,* Bergh Edition, Jefferson Memorial Association, Washington, D.C., 1907, vol. 17–18, p.425.

tion had increased to about 100,000. With the coming of the great Irish and German migrations of the 1840s and 1850s the Catholic population reached 2 million. Anti-Catholicism, never far from the surface, now engulfed a large portion of the nation. "No Popery" became the battle cry of such men as Samuel F. B. Morse and the Reverend Lyman Beecher. Catholic convents and churches were burned in New York, Boston, Philadelphia, and Newark. While the Protestant crusade of the 1840s and 1850s was as much antiforeign as it was anti-Catholic, nonetheless it drove a deep wedge between Protestants and Catholics in America.

The Catholic populations naturally resented the more vicious forms of bias practiced by the Know Nothings and the American Protestant Union. The most sensitive area of conflict, then as now, was centered around public education. When the great mass of Catholics arrived in the United States they found a public school system which was thoroughly Protestant in all respects. Catholic children were required to read the Protestant version of the Bible, sing Protestant hymns, and recite Protestant prayers, and history was taught with a Reformation bias. The extent of this influence can be seen in New York City. A Protestant group known as the Public School Society acquired a virtual monopoly of the public schools, operating them with public funds. There was a secular movement in public education but even the most secular-minded of all educational leaders, Horace Mann, considered indoctrination in the Christian religion a required part of public education. There is little doubt that Mann believed that the Christian religion was equivalent to interdenominational Protestantism.

While it is likely that there would have been some type of parochial school system, this Protestant domination of the public schools accelerated the movement.

At first the Catholics demanded a share of state school funds to support Catholic schools. When this was rejected the Catholics responded with a drive for the parish parochial school and increased their demands that the public schools become entirely secular in order to protect the Catholic children enrolled in them.

By the latter part of the nineteenth century and the early part of the twentieth, American Catholics under the leadership of Archbishops Ireland and Gibbons were assimilating into the American pattern of church-state relations. Above all, American Catholics accepted separation of church and state and religious liberty; indeed the Catholic Church thrived in America under separation. However, the Catholics had assumed an enormous financial burden in the parochial school system. The time would come when they would seek public assistance to relieve the burden.

THE PRACTICE OF SEPARATION: BUS TRANSPORTATION

In the spring of 1963 several hundred Catholic parochial school children in central Missouri forced their way onto public school buses, and when they reached the nearest public school they demanded to be enrolled. The Catholics were protesting the refusal of the Missouri Legislature to pass legislation reversing a Missouri Supreme Court decision that public support of parochial bus transportation was illegal. The incident was illustrative of the current battle being waged by Catholics to obtain some form of public support for the parochial school system.

By the early 1960s there were over five million children enrolled in Catholic elementary and secondary schools. They accounted for approximately 14 per cent of the total elementary and secondary school population in the United States. When the Catholic school children attempted to enroll in a few Missouri public schools in the spring of 1963 the Missouri state commissioner of education said that if the protest enrollments spread it would cause financial disaster to the state's school system.

In areas of high Catholic population, demands for indirect financial relief for parents of parochial school children have been made with increasing regularity within the last twenty-five years. A frequent demand has been for bus transportation. In 1941 New Jersey passed a permissive statute allowing local school districts to reimburse the parents of all school children for bus transportation. When the parents of parochial school children were given reimbursement the law was attacked as a violation of separation of church and state. The attack reached the Supreme Court in 1947.

In *Everson v. Board of Education,*[6] the Court took the opportunity to interpret "no establishment" in strong Jeffersonian terms. The Court stressed that neither a state nor the Federal government may pass laws which aid one religion or all religions or prefer one religion over another. Nor may the government levy any tax to support any religious activity or institution. Still, the Court was unwilling to strike down the New Jersey bus law. Relying on the earlier "child benefit theory,"

[6] *Everson v. Board of Education,* 330 U.S. 1 (1947).

the Court concluded that the bus aid was directed at the safety of the child and not to the benefit of a religion.

The child benefit theory had been previously used to uphold the constitutionality of a state law which provided free nonsectarian textbooks to all school children, parochial and public.[7] Textbook aid is currently supplied by West Virginia, Louisiana, and Mississippi and is under consideration in other states. It was declared in violation of the state constitution by the Oregon Supreme Court in 1961. The Oregon court rejected the Everson reasoning and the child benefit theory.[8]

Public bus transportation of parochial school children continues in hundreds of school districts throughout the nation. The courts in New York, Connecticut, Maryland, New Jersey, Kentucky, and California have all upheld the constitutionality of public support for parochial bus transportation. But the child benefit theory is under attack. It came under attack in the Oregon textbook case, and in 1962 the Wisconsin Supreme Court rejected it along with the *Everson* decision in a school bus transportation case. The Wisconsin court flatly held that bus aid benefited the religious schools and not the child.[9]

THE PRACTICE OF SEPARATION: RELIGIOUS OBSERVANCES AND INSTRUCTION

There is little question that the public school system is far more secular in the 1960s than it was one hundred years ago. On the other hand, the system has never totally divorced itself from the American religious heritage. Bible readings, Christmas plays, prayers, and hymns are accepted practices in many areas of the United States. At one time this was largely a Protestant influence, but as parochial schools lagged in development and more and more Catholic children attended public schools, the Catholics joined Protestant and Jewish groups in an effort to bring into the public schools optional sectarian instruction. This movement, known as the weekday church school program, began in 1914. One variant of the movement provided for the release of pupils during school hours to attend sectarian instruction within the school building. In 1948, the year following the bus transportation case, the United States Supreme Court had an opportunity to examine the released-time program.

[7] *Cochran v. Louisiana*, 281 U.S. 370 (1930).
[8] *Dickman v. School District 62–C*, 366 P.2d 533 (1961).
[9] *Wisconsin v. Nusbaum*, 115 N.W.2d 761 (1962).

In *McCollum v. Board of Education* the Court faced a situation where pupils had the option of attending religious instruction in the classroom or going to a study hall. The instruction was given by outside religious teachers and no public funds were used for the immediate purpose of the program. The Court held this to be in violation of the no establishment clause, primarily because it amounted to the use of tax-supported property for religious instruction, but also because of the close cooperation of the public school and the local religious council in promoting religion and because of the use of the compulsory education system to provide an audience for sectarian instruction.[10]

The *McCollum* decision was important, not so much because it struck down the released-time program, but rather because it was an indication of a growing sentiment of the Court, first noted in the *Everson* case, in favor of an absolutist position in church-state relations. Not only did the Court accept "no establishment" as equivalent to a high wall of separation but also the Court interpreted the gradual elimination of particular sectarian domination of public schools to mean that public education should be exclusively secular in operation and orientation.

The weekday church school movement had widespread support from Catholics, Protestants, and Jews. The *McCollum* decision went too far. Within four years, in 1952, the Court limited the impact of its decision by upholding a New York program for the dismissal of public school children during school hours to receive religious instruction at designated centers away from the public school.[11] The main element in the *McCollum* decision which was absent in this new dismissed-time decision was the use of tax-supported property, but the other elements of cooperation and captive audience were present, and the majority of the Court chose to ignore them.

However in 1959 the Washington State Supreme Court did not ignore the cooperation between the public school and the religious council. The state court held a dismissed-time program, which was the same as the New York program, to be in violation of the Washington constitution.[12] A dismissed-time program could hardly be successfully conducted without cooperation between a coordinating religious council and the public school authorities, and the Washington court saw the cooperation as equal to the use of public facilities to promote religion.

[10] *McCollum v. Board of Education*, 333 U.S. 203 (1948).
[11] *Zorach v. Clauson*, 343 U.S. 306 (1952).
[12] *Perry v. School District 81*, 344 P.2d 1026 (1959).

The dismissed-time program, while it has received some setbacks, is extensively practiced throughout the United States. In New York City alone over 100,000 children are excused one hour a week for religious instruction. In the face of this practice, to push the doctrine of separation as far as the Washington court did comes very close to indicating a hostility toward religion. Our constitutional system presupposes no such hostility. Nor is there a practical argument against such a program. Certainly the argument of religious pluralism presents no barrier to such an off-campus option program. As the United States Supreme Court said in the New York dismissed-time case, "When the state encourages religious instruction or cooperation with religious authorities by adjusting the schedule of public events to sectarian needs, it follows the best of our traditions." The Constitution cannot be callous toward religion; if it were it would prefer the nonbeliever over the believer.[13]

THE PRACTICE OF SEPARATION: PUBLIC SCHOOL PRAYERS AND BIBLE READINGS

A Southern Senator blasted, "They have taken God out of the schools and put the Nigras in." The occasion for this intemperance was a 1962 Supreme Court decision holding the New York State public school prayer unconstitutional. The brief and denominationally neutral prayer, a daily classroom exercise, read: "Almighty God, we acknowledge our dependence upon Thee, and we beg Thy blessing upon us, our parents, our teachers and our Country."

In anticipation of adverse public reaction the Court noted that to prohibit state laws respecting an establishment of religious services in the public schools did not indicate any hostility toward prayer or religion:

> It is neither sacrilegious or antireligious to say that each separate government in this country should stay out of the business of writing or sanctioning official prayers and leave that purely religious function to the people themselves and to those the people choose to look to for religious guidance.[14]

The reaction to the decision was loud and largely ill-considered. In Congress the decision was called "godless" and 30 constitutional amend-

[13] *Zorach v. Clauson,* 343 U.S. 306 (1952).
[14] *Engel v. Vitale,* 370 U.S. 421 (1962).

ments were introduced to reverse it. The proposed amendments had all the characteristics of token gestures of defiance to pacify constituents. The proposals died for lack of support in Congress.

The controversy did not end with the New York prayer case. In 1962, 40 states and the District of Columbia used Bible readings and prayers as a regular part of public school exercises. Indeed, 10 states even required by statute the recitation of prayers or Bible readings.[15] After the New York decision public schools continued to recite prayers and to read selections from the Bible. Some of the schools justified this by contending that the Court had only disallowed officially composed prayers.

In 1963 the Court disabused the public schools of this impression. In two companion state cases the Court, in an 8 to 1 decision, declared Bible readings and prayers as religious ceremonies in public schools in violation of the no establishment clause as applied to the states by the due process clause of the Fourteenth Amendment.[16]

In one of the cases a Pennsylvania law required the daily reading of at least ten Bible verses. The Edward Schempp family of Germantown brought an action against the law. The Schempps, as Unitarians, found the daily reading of the King James Bible and the recitation of the Lord's Prayer a trinitarian religious ceremony and as such contrary to their religious beliefs. The second case was instituted by an atheist Baltimore mother in behalf of her atheist son. The mother felt that religious ceremonies in the Baltimore schools placed a premium on belief as against nonbelief, thus making alien and sinister the moral values of the nonbeliever.

The 1963 decision was a return to the spirit of the *Everson* and *McCollum* decisions. In essence the Court asserted that in the matter of religion the state must be neutral, neutral in neither advancing nor inhibiting religion. It recognized that religion has a place in public education but not as religious ceremony. The legitimate place of religion in education could only be through the study of comparative religion, religious history, or Biblical literary studies presented in a secular and objective manner. In conclusion the Court observed that "the place of religion in our society is an exalted one, one achieved through reliance on the home, the church and the inviolable citadel of the individual heart and mind."

[15] Donald E. Boles, *The Bible, Religion, and the Public Schools,* The Iowa State University Press, Ames, Iowa, 1961, chap. 2.
[16] *Murray v. Curlett* and *School District of Abington v. Schempp,* 83 Sup. Ct. 1560 (1963).

The immediate public reaction to the decision was mixed but more temperate than reaction to the 1962 New York prayer case. The National Council of Churches, representing major Protestant leaders, felt that school prayers and Bible readings cheapened religion, particularly when used by school officials as a means of maintaining classroom discipline. The Synagogue Council of America, representing Orthodox, Conservative, and Reform Judaism also approved of the Court's action. Roman Catholics, who one hundred years ago had fought against these very practices, were divided, but the weight of opinion was against the decision. Monsignor John Voight, secretary for education of the Roman Catholic archdiocese of New York, felt the decision was wrong because it would foster secularism in public education and because it ignored the wishes of a majority of parents who favored religious practices. In this he was joined by Bishop Fred P. Corso of the World Methodist Council.

It is probably true that majority opinion has supported Bible readings and prayers, and hence the Supreme Court could be accused of thwarting majority rule. Yet democracy is not a simple problem in arithmetic. Democratic majority rule must be balanced by respect for minority rights. One of the basic purposes of our Bill of Rights is to keep the majority from imposing a tyranny, religious or otherwise, on the minority.

The prayer and Bible reading decisions: Compliance. The big question after 1962 was whether such long standing customs could be altered by judicial decisions. This author conducted a national random survey of public elementary school teachers during the academic year 1964–1965. The mail questionnaire was sent to 2,320 teachers and 1,712 responded. The results indicate that since the Court handed down its decisions there has been a noticeable shift in actual classroom practices.[17]

TABLE 3   MORNING PRAYERS BEFORE 1962

DAILY	WEEKLY	LESS THAN WEEKLY	NOT AT ALL
720	33	19	498

[17] Row totals do not equal 1712 either because respondents did not answer a question or because they were not teaching before 1962.

TABLE 4   MORNING PRAYERS 1964–1965

DAILY	WEEKLY	LESS THAN WEEKLY	NOT AT ALL
321	24	29	946

A similar shift occurred for classroom Bible readings:

TABLE 5   BIBLE READINGS BEFORE 1962

DAILY	WEEKLY	LESS THAN WEEKLY	NOT AT ALL
512	72	106	745

TABLE 6   BIBLE READINGS, 1964–1965

DAILY	WEEKLY	LESS THAN WEEKLY	NOT AT ALL
208	43	103	1261

While the above data indicate a significant national shift away from classroom prayers and Bible readings, the data also revealed that a majority of Southern respondents continued prayers and Bible readings.

BIRTH CONTROL: A NEW CONSENSUS

In 1879 Anthony Comstock, defender of Victorian morality, was successful in getting the state of Connecticut to adopt a law which attempted to regulate conduct in the most private of all areas, the bedroom. The Comstock law makes it illegal to use contraceptive devices. Until 1962 the law was ignored in the drugstores and bedrooms of Connecticut. However, a growing concern over the population explosion—three children are born every second—focused national attention on the Comstock approach to birth control. The government, on both the state and national levels, became involved in the problem, and governmental involvement in birth control has raised an issue in church-state relations. Three interrelated events occurred which demonstrate the religious issue in the current birth control problem.

The first event was the discovery and commercial marketing of an effective oral contraceptive pill. The Roman Catholic Church is opposed to artificial birth control, that is, to any method of birth control which violates natural law. Many of the most prominent spokesmen of the Catholic Church saw doctrinal objections in the use of the oral contraceptive pill. The second event was a concerted effort to get contraception, including the new pill, accepted as a legitimate part of public medicine in government-operated hospitals and clinics. The final event was the public controversy which resulted from this new birth control device.

Some form of birth control had become an accepted pattern in the upper and middle classes long before the discovery of the new pill. Yet effective birth control measures are not practiced by the economically and medically deprived groups in America. Most states do not interfere with private birth control measures. But many states do interfere with public birth control measures. Only two states, Massachusetts and Connecticut, have laws against the use of contraceptive devices, yet several states impose a variety of restrictions on the sale, distribution, and advertising of birth control devices.

In 1959 the Planned Parenthood Committee of Phoenix, Arizona, was prohibited from distributing any birth control literature in the publicly operated clinics and hospitals of Maricopa County. The county medical units did not provide birth control services, but until that date they had allowed the committee to distribute literature in the public clinics, and the staff doctors and nurses had referred mothers to the private clinic operated by the committee. This minimal cooperation was discontinued because of a 1901 Arizona statute which makes it a criminal offense to advertise or publish information about any medicine or means of preventing conception. The committe sought a court ruling to have the statute declared in violation of freedom of speech and press. The Arizona Supreme Court upheld the statute as a reasonable limitation on speech and press, asserting:

> In our estimation the statute could reasonably protect both the morals and the health of the community inasmuch as stimulation of sales of contraceptives might lead to greater sexual activity among unmarried persons.[18]

The court felt that the statute might discourage illicit sexual relations among young persons and thus prevent the spread of venereal disease. This was a rather monumental assumption on the part of the Arizona court and if it is wrong, that is, if the statute does not discourage illicit sexual relations, then the statute might have an entirely different impact on the problem of venereal disease. However, the court did say

18 *Planned Parenthood v. Maricopa County*, 375 P.2d 719 (1962).

that the statute only limited public advocacy of specific trade devices or preparations in the contraceptive field. It did not prohibit the policy of medical referrals or the dissemination of general literature by Planned Parenthood about birth control.

The Massachusetts and Connecticut laws have been violated privately with perfect impunity for many years. Until recently no one has ever been prosecuted in either state for using a contraceptive device. The laws did, however, act as an obstacle to any public birth control or family planning clinics. The Planned Parenthood League of New Haven decided to test the Connecticut law, and brought an action to have the law declared in violation of due process. The state court upheld the law and when the decision was taken to the United States Supreme Court the latter refused to decide the constitutional issue because no one had ever been prosecuted for violating it.[19] The New Haven Group then decided openly to challenge the law by opening a birth control clinic in 1962. When the clinic was opened the medical and executive directors of the clinic were promptly arrested and convicted for violating the Comstock act. The decision was appealed to the Supreme Court and the Court reversed the conviction, holding that a law forbidding the use of contraceptives invades a zone of privacy created by several constitutional guarantees. [20]

In the same year, 1962, another birth control controversy gained national attention. The issue arose in Chicago. In the Cook County Hospital there are 20,000 deliveries per year; most of them are babies of the poor, of Negroes and Puerto Ricans, and a sizable number are illegitimate. Many of the children and their mothers find their way onto the public relief roles of the Illinois Public Aid Commission. In 1962 there were 64,000 illegitimate children on the Illinois relief rolls; 28,000 were born after their mothers went on relief. The tax burden is high. The Aid for Dependent Children program in Illinois costs $93,600,000 annually. In spite of these social and economic facts, the Cook County Hospital does not include in its advice to maternity patients information on family planning or birth control measures. The position of the hospital has been that its patients may seek such information from private physicians but not from staff doctors. It claims that it does not have time to provide the information and that as a public hospital it has no right to determine who is to live or die. In

---

[19] *Poe v. Ullman*, 367 U.S. 497 (1961).
[20] *Griswold v. Connecticut*, 381 U.S. 479 (1965).

other words birth control is not an accepted part of public health, however much it is encouraged in private medicine. A more candid explanation would include the strong pressures from Roman Catholics against public artificial birth control.

Some contend that the absence of birth control information in public medicine makes second-class citizens out of those who cannot afford private medicine. The lower-income groups do not know where to go to get family planning information, and in reality there is no place for them to go. Public hospitals have been long on evasive answers and short on information.

In face of this situation the Illinois Public Aid Commission voted in December, 1962, to provide free birth control information to mothers, married or unmarried, who were on public relief. The commission vote was 6 to 4, with the four Roman Catholic members dissenting. The new program caused an immediate political storm. The vicar general of the Roman Catholic archdiocese of Chicago announced his opposition. One Catholic member of the commission resigned in protest, stating that the program would promote criminal sexual promiscuity. Protestant and Jewish groups endorsed the action of the commission. The Illinois attorney general denounced the program as immoral and illegal, and bills were introduced in the state Legislature to kill the program. In the late spring of 1963 the chairman of the commission was fired.

The New Haven and Chicago incidents point up a crucial issue in church-state relations: just how far should the state go in limiting its policy out of respect for the religious views of a substantial minority of the population?

The Massachusetts and Connecticut laws are of course unique, but they are also symbols. The laws were passed by Protestant-dominated legislatures in a burst of neo-Calvinism in the late nineteenth century. For their time they represented a consensus of opinion between Protestants and Catholics, a consensus which no longer exists. They have been kept on the statute books because of the political influence of Roman Catholics. Many Catholic theologians have little sympathy for the laws, not because they approve of contraceptive devices but because they disapprove of any state law which enters the bedroom. Yet to sanction their repeal might be interpreted in some quarters as approval of contraceptive devices. The laws remain then as symbols of Roman Catholic opposition to artificial birth control.

The important question is not whether the Massachusetts and Connecticut laws should be repealed or declared in violation of the First Amendment; the real question is whether the government should attack a population problem by any method which is morally offensive to Roman Catholics and to some fundamentalist Protestants. There is little question that it has been due to the political influence of Roman Catholics that medically approved birth control devices have been excluded from public health services. Furthermore there appears to be consensus among non-Catholics that artificial birth control is not morally objectionable. The time has come for Roman Catholics to ask themselves whether they should expect the state to enforce a moral code at odds with the sympathies of society at large. While Catholics must not be expected to change their moral convictions, nonetheless they should consider the wisdom of imposing on non-Catholics a Catholic moral position.

FEDERAL AID TO SECTARIAN SCHOOLS

The Constitution clearly prohibits aid to the . . . parochial schools. I don't think there is any doubt about that.

> President John F. Kennedy, March 1, 1961

I am . . . opposed to any program of Federal aid that would penalize a multitude of America's children because their parents choose to exercise their constitutional right to educate them in accordance with their beliefs.

> Francis Cardinal Spellman, March 13, 1961

And so ended Federal aid to education in the early 1960s.

President Kennedy, true to his Houston address, refused to include even indirect or auxiliary aid to sectarian schools in his 2.5-billion-dollar education bill in 1961. Cardinal Spellman, true to his long-standing position, marshaled Roman Catholic opposition to the bill. In July, 1961, the administration bill died in the House Rules Committee by a vote of 8 to 7. The key vote was that of Rep. James J. Delaney. He was joined by five Republicans and two Southern Democrats. Delaney is a Roman Catholic. Two other Roman Catholics on the committee voted in favor of the bill.

The Catholic position: Unequal burdens and equality of the law. Basically the Catholic position on Federal aid is that Catholics are currently being denied natural or distributive justice in the double taxation imposed on them in educating their children. Catholics and non-Catholics alike agree that it is a constitutional, indeed, a natural right, of all parents to supervise the education of their children.[21] Some parents have chosen to exercise this right in public schools, and others have elected to send their children to schools which include religious training. There is nothing inherently logical in the position that merely because a majority have elected the state-operated school system therefore all the tax monies in education must go to that system. Why should the Catholics forfeit their due share of the public funds which they contributed to and which have been set aside for education merely because they choose a different method of exercising the same constitutional right which the parents of public school children are exercising? It is clearly inequitable to place a penalty on the exercise of a constitutional right. No such penalty is found in Canada, Great Britain, Germany, Holland, or France where the state does aid the church schools.

It should also be noted that when Catholic bishops opposed the Kennedy proposals in 1961 they were not asking the government to treat parochial schools and public schools in exactly the same manner. The National Catholic Welfare Conference merely requested that parochial schools not be excluded from indirect aid in the form of long-term, low-interest Federal building loans. Catholic colleges were already the recipients of dormitory loans under the Federal Housing Act of 1950.

From a constitutional position there is little question that indirect aid aimed at the nonsectarian aspects of parochial education, such as science laboratories, and auxiliary services aimed at the benefit of the child, such as the Federal hot lunch program or bus transportation, are not prohibited by the Constitution. The Supreme Court stated as recently as 1952 in *Zorach v. Clauson,* "The First Amendment does not say that in every and all respects there shall be a separation of Church and State." [22]

To say, as President Kennedy did, that the Constitution clearly prohibits aid is to give an exceedingly mechanistic interpretation of the First Amendment. The no establishment clause, like most clauses in

---

[21] *Pierce v. Society of Sisters,* 268 U.S. 510 (1925).
[22] *Zorach v. Clauson,* 343 U.S. 306, 312 (1952).

the Constitution, is merely a foundation, and to turn it into an absolute formula begs the real question of whether such aid is wise public policy.

The non-Catholic position. When the Roman Catholics point out that they are educating well over five million elementary and secondary school children at a considerable financial sacrifice, the non-Catholic is apt to reply that the Catholics chose to make the sacrifice, that it was not imposed on them by the state. The American Civil Liberties Union stated the case thus:

> Every American is free to send his child or children to the public schools . . . or, alternatively, to send them to a church-controlled school. It has been urged in the name of "distributive justice" that parents who wish to send their children to religious schools are penalized for the "free exercise" of their religion. . . . But all citizens must be prepared to pay in one way or another for their convictions or preferences.

Still, the fact that a Catholic parent has a choice does not explain why the preference should carry an additional price.

There are a multitude of reasons why the non-Catholic expects the Roman Catholic to pay the additional price. The colonial heritage of anti-Catholicism still lingers on in America. There are suspicions among such groups as Protestants and Others United for Separation of Church and State about the political philosophy of the Catholic Church, about its seeming antidemocratic attitudes, and about its willingness to step into the political arena in obvious power-bloc moves. There is also a degree of religious rivalry and distrust, a fear by Protestants and Jews that any aid to the parochial school will further the strength of the Catholic Church in America, a strength they already fear. There is also a deep and abiding conviction that the parochial school system is a divisive element in our society and should not be encouraged. To many Americans the public school is the place and indeed the best place for young Americans to learn about democracy, about social tolerance and class fluidity. Thus the non-Catholic, while willing to allow the parochial system to exist, does not feel that an institution which shields the child from competing ideologies and values should be developed with state funds.

To the defenders of the religious school this latter argument is strange in a society committed to pluralism. If diversity is desirable in a democracy then why discourage the church school? To discourage the church school can only lead to a conformity which is already deeply entrenched in the public schools. This response, however, avoids an important question. The present balance between public and private education does result in diversity, but once state support of sectarian education begins will this balance and diversity continue?

Shared time: Creative compromise? In the current debate over state aid to sectarian education an old program has gained new prominence—shared time. For over thirty years in cities such as Evanston, Illinois, and Hartford, Connecticut, parochial school children have shared public secondary school facilities in home economics, industrial arts, physics, and chemistry. Under this program, church school children attend the public secondary school at certain hours during the week to receive instruction and training in secular fields, particularly fields which would require extensive investment by the church school in space and equipment. By the spring of 1963 the program was in operation in some school districts in 26 states. It has been urged by some that shared time be expanded as a compromise to the state-aid issue.[23]

The program's greatest advantage would be financial relief for the church school, particularly the Catholic schools. Many Catholic educators realize that unless the financial burden on the parochial school system eases the percentage of Catholic children enrolled in public schools will continue to increase. The shared-time program would also give the parochial student common experiences with the public school student. Such integrated educational experiences would help to produce a greater feeling of tolerance and understanding. Furthermore, Catholic taxpayers would be given a greater interest in promoting public schools, particularly at the time of school bond elections. Finally, it would ease church-state strife by a method which appears to be constitutionally sound. Strife would be eased in two ways: first, by freeing the public schools from demands for sectarian influences and instruction, and second, by reducing demands for public aid to sectarian schools.

The program is not without disadvantages. It would complicate curriculum time schedules and increase the administrative and financial

[23] "Symposium: Shared Time," *Religious Education*, January, 1962, pp. 5–36.

burdens of the public schools. Additionally, the program could not be adapted to elementary education, and thus would provide only indirect relief for the greatest number of church schools. The indirect relief would come only to the extent that the parochial school funds in the secondary area could be diverted to elementary schools. Finally, any extensive adoption of the program would not only help Catholic schools, it would also encourage the growth of the relatively small Protestant and Jewish schools and thus weaken the public school system.

The Elementary and Secondary Education Act of 1965. The deadlock in Federal aid to education was broken in 1965 when the National Education Association, long an opponent of state aid to church schools, and the National Catholic Welfare Conference agreed to endorse President Johnson's Federal education bill. The success of the bill was largely the result of focusing the benefits of the legislation on the children of low-income families.

While the legislation does not mention shared time, it does speak in Title I of the dual enrollment of public and private school children and the 1965 administrative regulations implementing the new legislation provides for the sharing of personnel and equipment between private and public schools. However, the regulations also provide that the control over personnel and equipment will be vested only in a public agency.

Children in nonprofit private schools also benefit under Titles II and III of the act. These titles provide for the purchase of instructional materials, such as textbooks, and for supplementary facilities, such as physical education and remedial instruction. In order to avoid a possible church-state conflict the act stipulates that title to all materials purchased under the act shall remain in a public agency.

While the National Catholic Welfare Conference estimated in 1966 that over 80 per cent of the diocesan school systems were participating in new Federally aided programs, the actual extent of the participation appeared to be quite minimal. This participation has not gone unchallenged by those who believe that such programs trangress the First Amendment.

There can be little dispute that parochial school children will benefit from the act. Whether parochial schools per se are the beneficiaries is not a question which can be determined objectively. There are 6,000,000 children enrolled in Catholic parochial schools, many of whom come from low-income families. The question which the judiciary may be called upon to decide is whether an otherwise valid government welfare program can be challenged when its benefits extend to children in a sectarian atmosphere.

CONCLUSION: The twentieth century has witnessed an extensive campaign to eliminate sectarianism in state action. In part this is due to the growing numbers of Jews and nonbelievers who, for different reasons, find it offensive for the state to foster or participate in religious life. Furthermore, the tendency of Protestantism to multiply into sects has strengthened the argument that in a religiously plural society it is impractical for the state to play an active role in the religious life of the community. However, in pressing a neo-Jeffersonian position, the advocates of separation have tended to demand that the wall of separation be raised to absolute heights. Such a position ignores the fact that "no establishment" and religious liberty should be complementary not contradictory rights. Separation was intended to serve religious liberty, not to do it a disservice. Freedom of religion and separation are a continuum; if either is pressed too far the other will suffer.

Review Questions

1. What is the child benefit theory? How has it been used by the courts?

2. What is the difference between "released time" and "dismissed time"? Which has the Court found to be constitutional? Which unconstitutional? What seems to be the critical factor in the decision?

3. Do schools in your community conduct classroom prayers? If so and if you felt this was in violation of "no establishment" what could you do to stop it?

4. What are the Comstock laws? Why are they difficult to enforce?

5. In the Arizona *Planned Parenthood* case, how did the court justify the restriction of free speech and press imposed by the anti-birth control statute?

6. What is really the crucial question raised by the birth control controversy and Catholic opposition to public birth control measures?

7. What did President Kennedy think about Federal aid to parochial schools? Do you think this position was justified?

8. What are the advantages and disadvantages of shared time for the Catholic and public schools?

THE SUPREME COURT, CRIMINAL JUSTICE, AND THE STATES

Chapter 5

SCOTTSBORO JUSTICE

On August 25, 1952, Haywood Patterson died in a Michigan prison. Patterson was serving a six-year to fifteen-year sentence for manslaughter. He had been convicted of stabbing a man in a Detroit barroom brawl. His death recalled an ugly chapter in American life. Haywood Patterson was a Scottsboro boy.

On March 25, 1931, two young "Southern ladies" dressed in overalls and wearing bobbed hair rode into Alabama from Chattanooga on a "side-door Pullman." On the same freight train were an assortment of Depression-born hobos, young white and Negro boys who were riding the rails in search of jobs. A fight occurred when the white boys demanded a Jim Crow freight train; they lost and were forced off the train. When the sheriff in the next town was informed of this he took a posse out to the station and arrested the Negro boys. However, when the sheriff discovered the hobo girls on the train he pressured them into stating that the Negro boys had raped them. The boys, all illiterate, were taken to the county seat, Scottsboro, and when a mob threatened to lynch them they were taken by the state militia to Gadsden. They were held in Gadsden until they were brought to trial in Scottsboro on April 6, 1931.

Scottsboro is the county seat of Jackson County. In 1931 it was a predominantly white farming community in the northern hill country of Alabama. Life in Jackson County was bleak and hard. The illiteracy rate was high, 40 per cent of the farms were mortgaged, and the tenancy rate was 60 per cent. There were few tractors, a lot of mules, and homes with telephones and electricity were scarce. When the news circulated throughout the county that nine "niggers" were being held for raping two white girls the air was filled with excitement. All the resentments and frustrations of Depression life in a rural community became focused on nine Negro boys. There was nothing like a good lynching to make the men forget about mortgages, foreclosures, taxes, and the wasted opportunities of a decade that passed them by. Scottsboro took on a festive air. Jim Crow justice was about to have a day in court.

On April 6, the trial date, the population of Scottsboro, normally around 2,500, swelled to 10,000. The country folk came in to swap mules and horses and to see the "niggers." A local band marched around the town playing "Dixie" and the state militia added a true martial spirit with the changing of the guard in front of the county courthouse, a courthouse which by now had machine gun emplacements.

The trial lasted one day. All the defendants pleaded not guilty. When the court discovered that they were unrepresented by counsel, the judge, in a cavalier manner, appointed all members of the local bar present in the courtroom to represent the boys. At the end of the day they were found guilty and eight of them were sentenced to die in the electric chair.

Within one month the United States Supreme Court agreed to review the convictions to see if any of the Federally protected rights of the defendants had been violated. Throughout the summer and early fall rallies were held across the nation to generate public support for the defendants. The Supreme Court was to announce its decision in early November.

On November 7, 1932, just one day before Franklin D. Roosevelt was elected President, 2,000 Negroes gathered in Birmingham to rally in support of the boys. November 7 was decision day in Washington in the Scottsboro case. The Birmingham rally broke up, however, when the Klan scattered pamphlets around announcing:

> Negroes of Birmingham, the Ku Klux Klan is watching you. Tell the communists to get out of town. They mean only trouble for you, for Alabama is a good place for good Negroes and a bad place for Negroes who believe in racial equality.

It was probably not unnatural for the Klan to look to the Communist agitators as the source of Negro discontent. However, in thirty years, the successors to the Klan, the White Citizens' Council. would begin to realize that the true source of at least part of the Negro stirrings could be traced back to the fateful week in November, 1932, when Franklin D. Roosevelt ushered in the New Deal and the Supreme Court of the United States began its historic probe into Jim Crow justice. The Court reversed the convictions, holding that the defendants had been denied due process of law when the state failed to provide them with counsel for defense.[1]

However, the Supreme Court's reversal of a conviction does not ensure that justice will be done. The Supreme Court operates in a federal system. It can request that a new trial be granted, as was done in the Scottsboro case, but it cannot guarantee that the new trial will be fair. After the first trial Haywood Patterson went through three additional trials for the same alleged offense. It is questionable if justice was done. He was finally convicted in 1936 and sentenced to seventy-five years' imprisonment. Of the remaining eight defendants, five had their indictments nol-prossed by the state, although one of the five was sentenced to twenty years for stabbing a deputy during the trial. Two other defendants were sentenced to seventy-five years and ninety-nine years each, and the ninth defendant was sentenced to death. This death sentence was commuted to life imprisonment. Patterson escaped from prison in 1948 and fled to Michigan. In 1951 he was convicted by a Michigan court for stabbing a man in a Detroit barroom brawl.

[1] *Powell v. Alabama*, 287 U.S. 45 (1932).

Of course, one could conclude that the young man who was killed in the Detroit barroom incident might still be alive today had Patterson been kept in prison. Undoubtedly a lot of people in Alabama and throughout the South felt vindicated when a Northern court sentenced Patterson to imprisonment. They knew all the time that Patterson was "a bad nigger." On the other hand one might also conclude that the young man would never have been killed if Haywood Patterson had never been arrested on a trumped-up charge and convicted in sham trials and brutalized and dehumanized in Alabama prisons for over sixteen years for a crime he never committed.

The prosecutions of the Scottsboro boys were not conducted as a search for criminal justice; rather they were manhunts in search of vengeance. Criminal justice means legally organizable morality. To some extent this morality will remain an aspiration and not a reality; to some extent there will always be a gap between the *is* of criminal practice and the *ought* of criminal justice. But the whole fabric of justice is endangered when the legal system, through the courts and law-enforcement agencies, fails to narrow the gap. Failure here results in Scottsboro justice.

FEDERALISM AND STATE CRIMINAL JUSTICE

Justice Cardozo, in discussing the nature of judicial decision making, observed:

> . . . Justice or moral value is only one value among many that must be appraised. . . . Other values, not moral, values of expediency or of convenience or of economic or cultural advancement, a host of values that are not final, but merely means to others, are to be ascertained and assessed and equilibrated, the less sacrificed to the greater. . . .[2]

Thus, when we examine the role of the Federal Supreme Court in state criminal justice we must be constantly aware that the judiciary consciously weighs values other than moral values in arriving at a decision in a case. Uppermost in the consciousness of the judiciary are the values of federalism and the effective and efficient enforcement of criminal law. An individual judge knows that his decision in a criminal

[2] Benjamin Cardozo, *The Paradoxes of the Legal Science*, Columbia University Press, New York, 1928, pp. 54–55.

case must satisfy the needs of society as a whole. Our civilized society presupposes the maintenance of good order. To preserve this good order, law-enforcement agencies must not be unduly hampered by judicial rules in the investigation and prosecution of crimes.

Furthermore, a Federal judge must always be mindful of the political reality of our federal system. Regardless of how antiquated some might feel the system to be, it is still a potent force in criminal law. The states have the primary responsibility for maintaining order on a daily basis, and under this system they are at liberty to develop their own criminal procedures and have done so. Our constitutional system of reserved powers for the states, while greatly altered in the last seventy-five years, still presupposes that the states have inherent powers in criminal prosecution. But the same Constitution which outlines a federal system also contains an amendment, the Fourteenth, which was probably intended to weaken the system of reserved powers. It was to this amendment that the Supreme Court turned in 1932 in the first Scottsboro case.

The Fourteenth Amendment, adopted in 1868 as a Civil War amendment, stipulates that no state shall deny to any person life, liberty, or property without due process of law and no state shall deny to any person the equal protection of the laws. In the aftermath of the Civil War the Supreme Court all but forgot about these clauses. It refused to tax Federal-state relations by interpreting them in such a way as to irritate the already strained relations between the central government and the states.[3]

For nearly sixty years after the adoption of the Fourteenth Amendment, the Court cast a suspicious eye on claims of denials of due process and equal protection of the laws in state criminal cases. During those sixty years the Court seldom reviewed a state criminal case and when it did the review was *pro forma*.[4]

Gradually the Court reexamined its earlier position. Undoubtedly this reexamination was due, in part to the failure of many of the states to develop adequate procedures to ensure that reason and not prejudice and passion guided the courts and law-enforcement agencies in criminal cases. Since the early 1930s the Court has become an active force in state criminal justice. The Court has intruded in the areas of arrest, search, and seizure, in the matter of coerced confessions, in jury selec-

[3] See *Hurtado v. California*, 110 U.S. 516 (1884); cf. *Moore v. Dempsey*, 261 U.S. 84 (1923).
[4] For example, *Frank v. Mangum*, 237 U.S. 309, 326 (1915).

tion, in counsel for defense. Until recently the Court has been hesitant to impose on the states the same procedural restrictions which are imposed on Federal law-enforcement agencies and Federal courts.

Beginning in the 1930s the Court attempted to get the states to follow the principle of "fair trial." [5] As used by the Court fair trial was a concept of minimal justice. When the Court was confronted with a set of facts alleging a denial of criminal due process by a state, it asked whether the alleged violation was one of those "fundamental principles of liberty and justice which be at the base of all our civil and political institutions." [6] Under this approach to due process the Court becomes endowed with the power periodically to examine state procedures to see if they conform to what the Court considers at a given time to be the "fundamental principles of liberty and justice." Thus, the due process clause became the conscience clause of the Constitution and the Court acted as the guardian of this conscience. One might have had no quarrel with this natural law approach to due process, an approach which made the members of the Supreme Court "priests of justice"; however, one can legitimately question whether the Court was quick enough to perceive the developing conscience of society in the area of criminal justice.

We now turn our attention to some specific problems in state criminal justice. The problems discussed are by no means exhaustive of current issues. They have been selected as examples of the effectiveness or ineffectiveness of the Supreme Court in promoting criminal justice in the context of our federal system.

COERCED CONFESSIONS

In 1628 Charles I gave his royal assent to a parliamentary petition which he considered revolutionary in tone. This Petition of Right acknowledged that no free man would be "detained in prison without cause shown." Since that date, many free men have been "detained in prison without cause shown." Nonetheless, as a free society we acknowledge the abstract right of a person to be free from illegal police detention. In theory when an individual is detained by the police he has the right to be taken before a magistrate promptly and arraigned on a charge. If there is no foundation to the charge the magistrate is obliged to release the individual. Such, at least, is the theory of a free society. Yet there are few procedural rights more commonly abused

[5] *Palko v. Connecticut*, 302 U.S. 319 (1937).
[6] *Herbert v. Louisiana*, 272 U.S. 312 (1926).

in the United States than the freedom from illegal police detention and the right of prompt judicial arraignment. The reasons for the abuse are not difficult to discover. All liberties have their counterbalancing forces. In 1628 Charles I pressed such a force in a letter to the House of Lords. He said that the "safety of the state" demanded from time to time the power of emergency administrative detention. He promised not to abuse the power. Law-enforcement agencies throughout the United States are at one with Charles. They also promise not to abuse the power. Their contention, which has merit, is that many murders, rapes, and robberies would go unsolved and unpunished without the power of secret interrogation to secure confessions of guilt.

Nearly all the states have statutes which require the prompt production of a person arrested. These statutes stipulate that all persons arrested be produced forthwith before a magistrate for arraignment or preliminary hearing. But compliance with prompt arraignment laws would in most cases deny the police the time and secrecy they want. Such compliance with the law would bring the accused before a judge, who would advise the accused of his right to silence. It would also likely bring counsel for defense. These two events would in all probability end any chance the police might have had for securing an immediate confession of guilt. In other words, compliance would reduce the likelihood of the "third degree."

The overwhelming majority of the American people never come into contact with criminal law enforcement. To the average person the third degree is quite remote. The public assumes that in the enlightened era of the 1960s such police conduct is so rare as to be truly insignificant. Yet a great deal of modern police practice in criminal investigations is built around illegal detention. In fact, in 1956 Los Angeles Police Chief William Parker told a congressional committee that, if the Supreme Court tried to impose on the states an effective prompt production requirement, modern law enforcement would be destroyed.

Police Chief Parker was talking about the Federal McNabb-Mallory rule. This rule, devised by the Supreme Court and imposed on all Federal law-enforcement agencies, provides that no Federal court may allow the introduction of a confession of guilt which was secured during a period of illegal detention. The Federal courts have operated under this rule for nearly twenty years and modern law enforcement on the Federal level has not been destroyed because of the rule.

It is impossible to give any accurate data on the precise extent of illegal police detention, nor is it possible to give accurate data on the extent of coerced confessions in the states. It is possible to make an intelligent guess. In the period from January 1, 1961, through May, 1962, there were over 75 cases decided in the highest courts of criminal appeal in the 50 states in which the defense alleged police coercion in securing the confession. Only 10 of these cases were reversed by the high state courts on the ground of coerced confessions. However, in an overwhelming number of the 75 cases the confession was secured during a period of illegal detention accompanied by substantial evidence of coercive police practices. Over 75 cases for 50 states in an eighteen-month period might not seem too significant. But when one considers that these were only the cases in the highest courts of appeal, then the figure takes on added weight. The Supreme Court has for some time recognized that a problem does exist. Since 1937 the Court has been developing a rule which forbids the use in a state criminal proceeding of a confession that was coerced or involuntary.

The subjective test. Between 1936 and 1964 the Supreme Court handed down 36 opinions in state coerced-confession cases. Throughout these cases the Court indicated a distaste for the third degree, an abhorrence of coerced confessions. Yet the Court was unwilling to read into the due process clause an effective solution to the problem, contending, instead, that "experience has confirmed the wisdom of our predecessors in refusing to give a rigid scope to this phrase." [7] On the contrary, the Court developed few absolutes in this area. It declared itself in favor of a subjective, case-by-case, fact-situation-by-fact-situation approach to the determination of coercion rather than imposing on the states the McNabb-Mallory rule.

One of the few absolutes maintained by the Court was announced in its first case in 1936. Here the Court asserted that "the rack and torture chamber may not be substituted for the witness stand." [8] But physical torture is so revolting to our sense of justice that its use by police is assumed by most to be an aberration.

A more common situation in a confession case is the use of fear, threats, or promises to compel a confession. For example, the police might strongly hint that unless a confession is made they will arrest close members of the accused's family or that unless the accused confesses the police will be unable to protect him from the awaiting mob.[9]

[7] Justice Frankfurter in *Malinski v. New York*, 324 U.S. 401, 414 (1945).
[8] *Brown v. Mississippi*, 297 U.S. 278 (1936).
[9] *Harris v. South Carolina*, 338 U.S. 68 (1949); *Payne v. Arkansas*, 356 U.S. 560 (1958).

As in the case of physical violence, a confession produced by fear, threats, or promises by the police is forbidden.

The use of fear and threats in combination with a variety of other police measures form what is today called a "psychologically coerced" confession, a confession by the third degree. Such a confession has a typical sequence of events: dragnet methods of arrest without a warrant and protracted and secret interrogation by relays of policemen in a jail where the accused is denied the benefit of counsel and friends and where judicial arraignment is so delayed as to make a mockery of the legal requirement.[10]

Under the subjective test approach the Court examined the "total circumstances" of the case to determine if a confession was a product of an essentially free and unconstrained choice by its maker. The total circumstances of a case included the actual conduct of the police in securing the confession and salient personal factors in the background of the accused, such as age, education, and emotional and mental stability. The weakness of the test was that it provided no substantial yardstick for the states. State courts examined the 30-odd Supreme Court cases and found authority for affirming or rejecting almost any type of confession. The Court has rejected a confession which was spontaneously given at the moment of arrest, and yet it has sustained a conviction where the confession was made after 14 days of interrogation.[11] Nor is the record free of incongruities in the use of fear. The Court has reversed a conviction where the accused was naked during part of his interrogation,[12] but has sustained a conviction where the police placed the bones of the deceased in the lap of the accused.[13]

While it is true that in none of the above-noted cases were these single factors decisive, still the fact remains that this subjective test was of critical value only in a limited number of situations. In the average state confession case, this *ad hoc* approach allowed the state courts to evade the test by the simple expedient of relying on the cases where the Court was generous in its latitude and ignoring the cases where the Court was more rigid.

A Texas jailhouse. On the night of November 16, 1959, Wilma Selby was murdered in Houston, Texas. In the following month on December 12 at 9:30 P.M., a twenty-three-year-old Negro, James Collins,

---

[10] For example, *Chambers v. Florida*, 309 U.S. 227 (1940) and *Ashcraft v. Tennessee*, 332 U.S. 143 (1944).

[11] *Gallegos v. Colorado*, 82 Sup. Ct. 1209 (1962); *Lisenba v. California*, 314 U.S. 219 (1941).

[12] *Malinski v. New York*, 324 U.S. 401 (1945).

[13] *Lyons v. Oklahoma*, 320 U.S. 732 (1943).

was arrested without a warrant and questioned by police. Later that same night, he was placed in a cell and held there until December 14. He was then questioned again, given a polygraph test, and released at 6:00 P.M. In the following month on January 19, 1960, at 8:00 P.M., Collins was again arrested without a warrant by the Houston police. He was taken to Ranger headquarters and from there to Humble, Texas, some 12 miles away. Here he was arraigned before a magistrate on a charge of vagrancy under the fictitious name of Joe Smith. He remained in the Humble jail until the following afternoon, at which time he was returned to Ranger headquarters in Houston. Starting at 6:30 P.M. that evening Collins was questioned constantly by several police officers, and some time between 6:30 and midnight he made a statement, but not a confession. He was interrogated further and some time around 3:15 A.M., he began to make a confession of guilt. The interrogation continued until 7:00 A.M. At 9:00 A.M., he was arraigned.

Here then is an accused who made a confession after being twice arrested without a warrant, after being illegally arraigned on a false charge under a fictitious name, who was illegally held and questioned intermittently during a two-day period with the final interrogation continuing throughout the night. Of course, he had no legal counsel during this period. He was described by medical experts as of low intelligence, with an abnormally low tolerance for stress—a man who had the character of a three-to-six-year-old child. With the use of this confession, Collins was convicted of murder and sentenced to ninety-nine years' imprisonment. Did Collins receive due process of law? The highest court of criminal appeals in Texas said yes and sustained the conviction.[14] The United States Supreme Court denied Collins's petition for review.

What influence did Federal Supreme Court decisions have in this case? None? No, they had some influence. The Texas Court of Criminal Appeals was quite familiar with the Supreme Court confession cases, but it distinguished away every precedent which might restrict the latitude of the state and applied every precedent which would give the state wide latitude in confession cases. This one Texas case was typical of the minimal influence of the Supreme Court in guiding state law enforcement agencies and state courts in confession cases.

Is it not strange to realize that what happened in the *Collins* case would never be sanctioned as procedure inside a court of law? No

[14] *Collins v. Texas*, 352 S.W.2d 841 (1961).

judge would allow a prosecutor to become a persecutor, to wear down a defendant in a closed courtroom, with or without counsel for defense. Why then must society close its eyes to what has occurred in the pretrial stages? What happened to Collins is perhaps an "aberration" in our system of justice. That it should occur at all, let alone with some degree of regularity, is a grave problem for a free society.

This is not to suggest that the police be prohibited from questioning suspects. Such questioning is a necessary and desirable part of police work. To acknowledge the necessity of police questioning is not, however, the same thing as acknowledging the necessity for secret and illegal detention, where the prisoner is made ". . . the deluded instrument of his own conviction."[15]

Beginning in 1961 with the decision in *Mapp v. Ohio* [16] the Court has been attempting to close the gap between Federal and state practices in criminal procedures. In 1963 the Court held that the Sixth Amendment's requirement that in all criminal prosecutions the accused shall enjoy the right of defense counsel was now obligatory on the states by means of the Fourteenth Amendment. The Court also noted that the states were required to provide such counsel for indigent defendants.[17] In the following year the Court handed down its famous decision in *Escobedo v. Illinois.*[18] The *Escobedo* decision attempted to meet the problems voiced at the state and local level by police interrogation of suspects. The Court held that when an investigation by police is no longer a general enquiry into an unsolved crime but rather has begun to focus upon a particular suspect and the suspect has been taken into custody, the police must allow the suspect to consult with counsel.

The *Escobedo* decision and another 1964 case which applied the Fifth Amendment's no compulsory self-incrimination clause to the states [19] raised a considerable outcry among state law enforcement agencies. The Court was again accused of tying the hands of the police and of coddling criminals. The full import of the *Escobedo* decision was not made clear until 1966.

In 1966 the Court clarified its position on confessions, police interrogation, and counsel. In that year the Court reversed convictions in

15 2 Hawkins, *Pleas of the Crown*, 8th ed., 1824, 595.
16 See below, p. 123.
17 *Gideon v. Wainwright*, 372 U.S. 335 (1963).
18 *Escobedo v. Illinois* 378 U.S. 478 (1964).
19 *Malloy v. Hogan*, 378 U.S. 1 (1964).

four separate cases. Each case involved police interrogations, absence of counsel for defense, and subsequent confession. In its 1966 decision the Court stated that:

> . . . the prosecution may not use statements, whether exculpatory or inculpatory, stemming from custodial interrogation of the defendant unless it demonstrates the use of procedural safeguards effective to secure the privilege against self-incrimination. By custodial interrogation, we mean questioning initiated by law enforcement officers after a person has been taken into custody or otherwise deprived of his freedom of action in any significant way. As for the procedural safeguards to be employed, unless other fully effective means are devised to inform accused persons of their right of silence and to assure a continuous opportunity to exercise it, the following measures are required. Prior to any questioning, the person must be warned that he has a right to remain silent, that any statement he does make may be used as evidence against him, and that he has a right to the presence of an attorney, either retained or appointed. The defendant may waive effectuation of these rights, provided the waiver is made voluntarily, knowingly and intelligently. If, however, he indicates in any manner and at any stage of the process that he wishes to consult with an attorney before speaking there can be no questioning. Likewise, if the individual is alone and indicates in any manner that he does not wish to be interrogated, the police may not question him. The mere fact that he may have answered some questions or volunteered some statements on his own does not deprive him of the right to refrain from answering any further inquiries until he has consulted with an attorney and thereafter consents to be questioned.[20]

The *Miranda* decision did not raise so great an outcry as did the *Escobedo* decision, but state and local police and prosecuting officials

[20] *Miranda v. Arizona*, 86 Sup. Ct. 1602 (1966).

were critical of the new requirements. These new standards may well result in some felons' going free. It is unlikely, however, that the requirements will actually contribute to an increase in crime. David Acheson, a former United States district attorney, observed, "Changes in court decisions and prosecution practices would have about the same effect on the crime rate as an aspirin would have on a tumor of the brain."

WIRETAPPING AND EAVESDROPPING

Back in the horse and buggy days of 1890 a promising Boston attorney by the name of Louis D. Brandeis wrote an article warning that modern scientific advances were seriously threatening the right to privacy. Brandeis, with uncanny clairvoyance, asserted that ". . . numerous mechanical devices threaten to make good the prediction that 'what is whispered in the closet shall be proclaimed from the house-tops.' " [21] On December 28, 1951, California police surreptitiously entered the home of Patrick Irvine and placed a microphone in Mr. and Mrs. Irvine's bedroom closet. With the aid of this eavesdropping device the police were able to listen to Irvine's telephone conversations. The police did not even bother to tap the telephone, as they had their own instruments placed inside the home. On the basis of information obtained from this illegally planted listening device, the police were able to obtain a gambling conviction against Mr. Irvine. The United States Supreme Court declared this to be a shocking and flagrant violation of privacy, but refused to upset the state conviction.[22]

During the prohibition era when rum running was a big-time business four "G-men" gained entry into the basement of a Seattle office building. The Federal officers tapped the telephone wires of one of the biggest gin businesses on the West Coast. The officers listened to telephone conversations for several months and then armed with this wiretap evidence they arrested Roy Olmstead and his partners. Olmstead's 2-million-dollar business collapsed, and one of the major law-enforcement controversies of the twentieth century began.

Olmstead's case ultimately reached the Supreme Court. He claimed that wiretapping was a violation of the Fourth Amendment and that under the Weeks rule the evidence should be suppressed. The Court rejected this contention and held that unless there is an actual physical

[21] Brandeis and Warren, "The Right to Privacy," *Harvard Law Review*, vol. 4, pp. 193, 195, 1890.
[22] *Irvine v. California*, 347 U.S. 128 (1954).

invasion of a constitutionally protected area, such as the home or office, the Fourth Amendment affords no protection.

The distinction which the five-man majority tried to make between tangible invasions of property or effects and wiretapping was at best mechanistic. The obvious policy of the Fourth Amendment should be a reasonable protection of personal privacy. It is immaterial to the principle of privacy whether an officer unreasonably enters an office or home and seizes papers or whether he taps the telephone and secretly listens to all conversations with the expectation of gathering incriminating evidence out of the mouth of the unknowing suspect.

The promising Boston attorney, Brandeis, was now a member of the Supreme Court and he dissented from the majority opinion. Brandeis cautioned the Court against such a static view of privacy as the majority adopted and observed that the Court was reducing the Fourth Amendment to a lifeless and impotent formula. Justice Holmes joined Brandeis in his dissent and warned against the government becoming a participant in "dirty business" for ". . . it is less evil that some criminals should escape than that the government should play an ignoble part." [23]

The Olmstead decision met with immediate attacks, but nonetheless law-enforcement agencies from the FBI down began to use wiretapping as a major weapon in criminal investigations. Finally in 1937 the Court reexamined the wiretapping issue. While the Court refused to reverse the decision it did take the sting out of it. For this purpose the Court seized upon section 605 of the Federal Communications Act of 1934. The pertinent provision of the section reads as follows: ". . . no person not being authorized by the sender shall intercept any communication and divulge or publish the existence, contents, substance, purport, effect or meaning of such intercepted communication to any person. . . ." In 1937 in the *Nardone* case the Court interpreted this language to mean that telephone wiretapping was prohibited.[24] Furthermore, the Court refused to allow illegal wiretap evidence to be used in Federal courts.

The wiretapping controversy did not end with the *Nardone* case. On the contrary, the controversy has increased over the years. Private wiretapping has continued, and police wiretapping on the Federal and state levels has not been greatly affected by the decision. The police refuse to live with the decision. Every United States Attorney General

---

[23] *Olmstead v. United States*, 277 U.S. 438, 470 (1928).
[24] *Nardone v. United States*, 302 U.S. 379 (1937).

since 1937 has backed legislation in the Congress to overturn the Nardone rule and give legal sanction to what the FBI has continued to do since 1937, i.e., to wiretap. Of course, the Justice Department is unable to use wiretap evidence in Court as a basis for a prosecution, but the Department has continued to tap telephone wires in investigations of national security cases, narcotic cases, tax cases, and gambling cases. The Department takes the position that wiretapping per se is not illegal under section 605, but rather it is illegal only when interception is coupled with divulgence. One must assume from this that the intercepting FBI operators never breathe a word of what they have heard. Nonetheless, when the FBI or other state and Federal officers have divulged the contents of wiretap conversations, they have not been prosecuted for violating the law.

In 1965 a Senate subcommittee held hearings on invasions of privacy by Federal agencies. During these hearings it was revealed that a number of Federal agencies including the Internal Revenue Service, the Customs Bureau, the Food and Drug Administration, and the Post Office were making use of various eavesdropping devices and wiretapping. The Senate investigation also uncovered the fact that the Federal government actually ran a school for Federal agents in the techniques of eavesdropping—the Treasury Technical Investigative Aid School. The school gave instruction in the techniques of wiretapping and electronic listening devices and lockpicking.[25]

The refusal of the highest law-enforcement officers of the Federal government to accept the ban on wiretapping has contributed to the widespread public and private disregard of the Court's position. At least in part the Court has contributed to this regrettable situation. While it does not appear likely that the Court will reverse its Nardone rule, it has consistently refused to broaden its application. Thus the Court has ruled that while the congressional prohibition against wiretapping applies to all persons, public and private, on both the state and Federal levels, they have refused to apply the judicially devised exclusion rule to the state courts.[26]

The reluctance of the Court to go beyond the ban established in the *Nardone* case is also apparent in its decisions in the closely related field of electronic eavesdropping. The Court has consistently held that detectaphones, miniphone recorders, and parabolic listening devices are

---

[25] *Hearings by the Senate Judiciary Committee*, "Invasions of Privacy," Government Printing Office, 1965.
[26] For example, *Schwartz v. Texas*, 344 U.S. 199 (1952).

not covered by section 605. The Court has even allowed telephone conversations to be introduced as evidence when the conversations were picked up by a delicate instrument placed on the office wall adjoining the defendant's office.[27]

At the present time the legal picture in wiretapping and electronic eavesdropping is intolerable to all sides. The Supreme Court is sitting on a judicial fence, the Congress has been unable to clarify the issue, and the states are left in doubt as to just what is and is not permissible. Six states, including New York, have statutes which allow judicially controlled wiretapping and/or eavesdropping. Yet the Court has observed that such statutes are in conflict with the supreme law of the land.[28] But the Court has indicated that it will not interfere with the permissive wiretap laws.[29] Thirty-three states, including Illinois, Pennsylvania, and California, have laws prohibiting wiretapping, although not all states enforce their prohibitions. Eleven states have no legislation. Some urban states, such as Illinois and Pennsylvania, have had active controls on wiretapping for the past five years, and no evidence has been forthcoming to indicate that law enforcement has suffered in these states from the lack of authority to wiretap. On the other hand, New York, particularly New York City, has consistently pressed the Federal government to repeal the Nardone rule and thus sanction its judicial wiretapping and eavesdropping laws. The New York courts continue to admit wiretap evidence.[30]

While both sides of the issue might agree that the present chaotic situation is intolerable, there is little agreement on a solution to the issue. The FBI annually pleads the necessity of wiretapping in national security cases, but then quickly adds that it should also be permitted in narcotic cases and gambling cases. State and local law-enforcement officers also testify annually before congressional committees about the necessity of wiretapping. It is argued that the United States faces an organized system of crime which threatens to become an invisible government and that in such a situation the right to privacy must yield where it can be shown that this right is being used to threaten the foundations of law and order. But testimony before congressional committees has also revealed that police convenience plays a significant role

[27] *Goldman v. United States,* 316 U.S. 129 (1942).
[28] *Benanti v. United States,* 355 U.S. 96 (1957).
[29] *Pugach v. Dollinger,* 365 U.S. 458 (1961).
[30] *Dinan v. New York,* 183 N.E.2d 689 (1962), certiorari denied, 83 Sup. Ct. 146 (1962).

in the pressure for legalized wiretapping. Police officials have been pressed into admitting that there are few, if any, criminal situations which inherently demand such investigatory methods. Rather it is a question of limited police budgets, lack of adequate forces, and a resort to the cheapest and quickest methods of detection.

Since the mid-1920s dozens of bills have been introduced and several hearings have been conducted to legalize limited wiretapping on the state and Federal levels. None has met with success. The proposals differ in many vital respects, but a common theme is the judicial wiretap warrant. Under this system a judge would issue a warrant upon probable cause to tap a telephone for a period of time. If wiretapping is to be legalized the judicial warrant system is to be preferred. However, in 1962 the Justice Department advocated an *executive* warrant system, a warrant to be issued by the Attorney General, in national security cases. The proposal carried forward the judicial warrant concept in murder, kidnap, gambling, bribery, narcotics, and interstate racketeering cases. Most of the proposals differ as to the duration of the tap order and the class of officers who might be able to seek the warrants. They all prohibit private wiretapping and usually they have some provision to allow the states to develop their own independent wiretapping systems.

The long legislative impasse in wiretapping and "bugging" appears to be an open invitation for the Supreme Court to reassert its Nardone rule with renewed vigor. It would be wiser for the Congress to pass legislation establishing a national policy for the Federal and state governments. But the issue has so fragmented power in the Congress that a legislative policy is not likely to be written in the near future. Such a situation is ripe for a judicial policy. The Court could strengthen the Nardone rule by applying it to the states, much as they have recently applied the Weeks rule to the states. In eavesdropping and bugging, they could adopt one of two alternative courses. They could reexamine eavesdropping as an illegal search and seizure issue or they could approach police bugging as a compulsory self-incrimination issue. The latter approach cannot be dismissed lightly. In a very real sense electronic bugging and recording can force an individual to incriminate himself against his will.

Such a judicial policy would not be a satisfactory solution to those who favor some wiretapping by the police. They argue that under the present chaotic system no one's privacy is really protected. They urge the adoption of legislation which the police would be willing to live with and which could be enforced. This is a shocking argument, a justification which attacks the foundations of our respect for law. The truth of the matter is that the Federal government has never really tried to enforce section 605 because it finds it inconvenient to do so.

There is no denying that some solution must be found. Science has outstripped the ability of the law to cope with the issue. But a rule of convenience is a dangerous foundation for a solution. A rule of convenience here would seriously jeopardize a cornerstone of our free society, and that is a reasonable respect by the state for the privacy of the individual. In a free society the individual must be able to close the door of his home with absolute assurance that the state will invade only under reasonable conditions. Certainly there are times when, in the broad interests of society, the government must be able to invade individual privacy and the Fourth Amendment anticipates such situations by providing for procedural safeguards. However, effective wiretapping by police could never meet an essential demand of the Fourth Amendment. This amendment never allows the state to secretly invade a private area. Even the most narrowly drawn and judicially controlled wiretap statute would never provide that the officers must tell the individuals concerned that their phones are to be tapped. Secrecy is the essence of a wiretap's usefulness. Yet when the state invades individual privacy it should be obliged to inform the individual of the invasion and announce the reasons for such. In wiretapping or eavesdropping situations this is impossible. The police cannot listen to some conversations on a given line and not to others, and to be effective they must listen in secrecy.

True, a total ban on wiretapping and eavesdropping would burden the police. But all procedural restrictions are irksome to the police and the prosecution. Moreover, procedural checks always interfere to some degree with the effectiveness of law enforcement. Still, if effectiveness in catching criminals is the principal standard by which we are to judge investigatory methods, then most individual rights will have to give way to effectiveness. There are many short cuts that could be taken in catching criminals, but a free society—in order to remain free —must risk the long way around.

RACIAL EXCLUSION AND THE JURY SYSTEM

Aubrey Williams, Negro, was tried and convicted by an all-white jury in March, 1953, for the murder of a white Atlanta liquor store operator. He was sentenced to die in the electric chair. Williams's jury was drawn from a box containing white and yellow tickets, one designating white persons and the other Negroes. Only three months after the Williams trial a similar Georgia case was reversed by the United States Supreme Court.[31] But Williams's lawyer had failed to challenge this discriminatory practice at the proper time, i.e., when the jury was put upon him. Instead, the lawyer attacked the method of jury selection after the trial. His case was appealed to the Supreme Court and that body refused to reverse the conviction. However, the Court did remand the case to the Georgia Supreme Court, noting:

> Fair regard for the principles which the Georgia courts have enforced in numerous cases and for the constitutional commands binding all courts compels us to reject the assumption that the courts of Georgia would allow this man to go to his death as a result of a conviction secured from a jury which the State admits was unconstitutionally impaneled.[32]

On remand the Georgia Supreme Court noted that it would bow to the United States Supreme Court ". . . on all federal questions but we will not supinely surrender sovereign powers of this State." [33] Shortly thereafter Aubrey Williams was executed in the electric chair.

Preston Cobb, Negro, lived with his widowed mother and some of his eight brothers and sisters in an unpainted tenant house on a farm in Jasper County, Georgia. In June, 1961, he was accused of murdering his white landlord. Preston was indicted and tried by an all-white jury and found guilty. But for his age, his case would have passed unnoticed. Preston Cobb was sentenced to die in the electric chair when he was fifteen years old. Cobb's youth brought international attention to the case. His white court-appointed attorney withdrew from the case immediately after the trial. The attorney had not raised the issue of racial exclusion at the trial, nor had he requested the jury to show mercy, nor had he filed a motion for a retrial. When he was interviewed the attorney stated that he had no intention of attacking ". . . the judgment of this fine jury of representative Jasper County citizens." [34] A "fine representative jury" which did not include one Negro and yet Jasper County's population was 53 per cent Negro!

The NAACP entered the case and appealed the decision to the Geor-

[31] *Avery v. Georgia*, 345 U.S. 559 (1953).
[32] *Williams v. Georgia*, 349 U.S. 375, 391 (1953).
[33] *Williams v. Georgia*, 88 S.E. 2d 376 (1955).
[34] *The New York Times*, Oct. 8, 1961, p. 52

gia Supreme Court. The Georgia court sustained the conviction, holding that Cobb's attorney, by failing to enter a timely objection to the jury list, had waived his client's right to object to the systematic exclusion of Negroes.[35] The United States Supreme Court refused to review the decision. In 1964 a Federal court of appeals granted Cobb a new trial and Cobb was subsequently retried in Jasper County and sentenced to life imprisonment.[36]

Unquestionably our adversary judicial system would encounter serious difficulties if the prosecution and the defendant were not held to the reasonable requirements of orderly procedures in the filing of motions. Normally it is entirely reasonable to expect the defense to raise the issue of racial exclusion in the jury list prior to trial. Otherwise the defense has the advantage of waiting for the verdict and if he does not like the verdict he can then ask for a new trial on the basis of racial exclusion. Nonetheless, it seems highly questionable whether it is proper to conclude that a fifteen-year-old Negro with an eighth-grade education in a capital case waived his rights to raise the issue merely because his court-appointed white lawyer failed to do so. As the United States Court of Appeals, Fifth Circuit, said in 1959:

> As judges of a circuit comprising six states of the Deep South, we think it is our duty to take judicial notice that lawyers residing in many southern jurisdictions rarely, almost to the point of never, raise the issue of systematic exclusion of Negroes from juries.[37]

Placing aside the questions of Cobb's age, the adequacy of his defense counsel, and his guilt or innocence, a major issue remains: Was Cobb discriminated against in his trial because of his race? The very fact of racial exclusion in the grand and petit juries creates a strong presumption Cobb did not receive equal justice. Only the most naïve would contradict the observation by the Supreme Court that "a Negro who confronts a jury on which no Negro is allowed to sit . . . might very well say that a community which purposely discriminates against all Negroes discriminates against him." [38] An all-white jury drawn from a racially biased list will in all probability mete out to a Negro defendant a more severe punishment than it would to a white defendant. A survey of state supreme court decisions for the years 1960 through

[35] *Cobb v. Georgia*, 126 S.E.2d 231 (1962).
[36] *Cobb v. Balkcom*, 339 F.2d 95 (1964).
[37] United States *ex rel. Goldsby v. Harpole*, 263 F.2d 71, 81 (1959).
[38] *Fay v. New York*, 332 U.S. 261, 293 (1947).

1962 indicates that in every murder case and in every rape case where the defendant was Negro and where the issue of racial exclusion was raised, the Negro defendant received the death sentence. Of course, these cases were only the ones which reached the highest courts of criminal appeals.

Between 1930 and 1957, 361 Negroes were executed in the South for rape in contrast to 38 whites. In Georgia Negroes accounted for 160 of the 200 executions between 1943 and 1964. Equal justice for the Negro or the Mexican-American will not be forthcoming from a racially biased jury. Racial exclusion is an "assertion of their inferiority, and a stimulant to that race prejudice which is an impediment to securing individuals of the race that equal justice which the law aims to secure to all others." [39]

The law of racial exclusion. In a series of decisions starting in 1880 the Supreme Court has consistently held that it is a violation of the equal protection of the laws clause of the Fourteenth Amendment for a state to exclude Negroes from jury service on the basis of race. Few positions of the Court in the area of civil rights have been more consistently clear. Not only has the Court viewed such exclusion as unconstitutional and the basis for a new trial, but there is even a Federal statute dating back to the days of Reconstruction that makes such exclusion a crime. No one has ever been convicted under the statute and yet violations of this right have repeatedly occurred over the past eighty years. In well over fifty cases, the Court has firmly established the following points:

1. If a Negro defendant can establish by evidence that members of his race have been excluded from jury service on the basis of race, there then results a presumption of discrimination.

   a. Such evidence must show that there were Negroes qualified to serve on the juries.

   b. The qualifications for jury service must not discriminate either covertly or overtly against Negroes as a class, e.g., the use of voter registration as a prerequisite when in fact Negroes are discriminated against in the county in voter registration.[40]

2. When the defense has created a prima-facie case of racial exclusion, then the burden is on the state to prove otherwise.[41]

3. No Negro is entitled to have members of his race on the jury which indicts him or tries him; he is merely entitled not to have

[39] *Strauder v. West Virginia*, 100 U.S. 303, 308 (1880).

[40] *Patton v. Mississippi*, 332 U.S. 463 (1947).

[41] *Neal v. Delaware*, 103 U.S. 370 (1881).

Negroes purposely excluded. Thus the mere absence of Negroes, without further evidence, creates no presumption of racial discrimination.[42]

4. The rules governing racial exclusion apply to class as well as race and color. Thus Mexican-Americans and presumably Puerto Ricans may raise the issue; however, the evidence must support the "separateness" of the class.[43]

5. The prohibition against racial exclusion applies to simple-minded as well as to ingenious devices which discriminate on the basis of race.[44]

Evasion of judicial standards. In spite of the repeated assertions of the United States Supreme Court and also of many Southern supreme courts, the white jury system continues to be a fortress of the rural South and only slightly less so in the urban South. The full explanation for this involves complex social, economic, and perhaps psychological forces which perpetuate race prejudice. A more immediate explanation is less complex. All-white jury lists continue to be used throughout the South for a variety of obvious reasons. The Negro defendant is frequently without legal counsel and consequently unaware of his constitutional rights. Where he does have counsel there is a reluctance to raise the issue out of fear of further prejudicing the court and the jury against the defense. Furthermore, the defense counsel must live in the community after the case is concluded.

Jury commissioners and court officials have frequently justified these all-white jury lists on the basis that they have no personal knowledge of qualified Negroes. However, the Supreme Court has warned the states that officials charged with compiling venire lists must execute their offices so as to familiarize themselves fairly with the qualifications of all eligible jurors. This has resulted, at least in the more serious felony cases, in placing the names of a few Negroes on the jury list. However, the Court has also warned that it is unconstitutional to limit Negro jurors to any given percentage of the list or to make the percentage of Negroes placed on the list correspond to the percentage of Negro population in the state or county. "Jurymen should be selected as individuals on the basis of individual qualifications, not as members of a race." [45]

Getting a few Negroes on the venire list is a far cry from placing

[42] *Ibid.*
[43] *Hernandez v. Texas,* 347 U.S. 475 (1954), and see *New York v. Agron,* 176 N.E.2d 556 (1961).
[44] *Avery v. Georgia,* 345 U.S. 559 (1953).
[45] *Cassell v. Texas,* 339 U.S. 282 (1950).

Negroes on the grand and petit juries. Where Negroes constitute a substantial portion of the population and where they have consistently appeared on the venire list, but never served on a jury, there is a strong presumption of racial discrimination. The end result cannot be attributed to chance or accident.

There are a number of reasons which explain the absence of Negro jury service when Negroes appear on the venire list. First, only a few appear on the list, i.e., the representation is token. Second, there is a rather widespread custom of a gentlemen's agreement between defense and prosecution not to accept Negro jurors. Third, both the prosecution and the defense have a limited number of peremptory challenges of prospective jurors which may be exercised capriciously. These challenges are frequently used to exclude the Negro. Recently the Supreme Court raised the possibility that in certain circumstances the use of peremptory challenges by the prosecution may violate the Fourteenth Amendment.[46] Additionally, each side has a right to make "challenges for cause," i.e., to challenge a prospective juror by showing a good reason why the individual could not render a fair verdict. Finally, Negroes are more likely than not to have just cause for exemption from jury service. The bulk of them are daily wage earners in the lowest income bracket, and jury service could be an economic hardship.

A recent Louisiana case illustrates the current problem. A Negro was charged with raping a white woman. The original list from which the petit jury was to be drawn contained 30 names, of which three were Negroes. But of the three, one was absent, one was challenged peremptorily, and one excused because of age. The first list was exhausted before a full jury was obtained and a second list of 50 names was used. This second list included seven Negroes, but one was excused because of illness, one challenged for cause, one challenged peremptorily, three claimed age exemption, and the seventh was absent. Again the list was exhausted and another list of 50 presented, which included eight Negroes. But a full panel was agreed to before the names of the eight Negroes were called. The all-white jury convicted the defendant and sentenced him to death.[47] The Negro population of the county was 6,000 as compared with 16,000 whites, or 27 per cent of the total population. Yet in the jury lists presented, the Negro percentages were, respectively, 10, 14 and 16 per cent. What this amounts to is token Negro representation on the jury of venire list and *de facto* exclusion from jury service.

[46] *Swain v. Alabama,* 380 U.S. 202 (1965).
[47] *Louisiana v. Clark,* 140 So.2d 1 (1962).

After eighty years of Supreme Court cases in this area there is little evidence to support any hope that a judicial solution to the problem is at hand. All the Court has been able to do is get a few Negroes on the initial jury list. If the judicial solution has been largely unsuccessful, what then can be done to ensure equal justice in jury selection? The Court might adopt a position which would hold all trials of Negroes by all-white petit juries and/or all-white grand juries in violation of the Constitution. Such a drastic change is not likely to occur, because it would require jury selection on the basis of race, a requirement inconsistent with the Fourteenth Amendment. The basic fact is that it is easy to evade judicial requirements in this area. Furthermore a judicial solution places the burden of combating the problem on Negro dedendants who will find it difficult to secure the necessary factual information to establish a case of prima-facie discrimination.

Another solution would be to enforce the one Federal criminal statute which makes racial exclusion by state officials a crime. Again, there is little hope for a successful solution. The statute has been on the books since 1875 and no one has been convicted of violating it. Its long disuse has sealed its fate. The lack of present solutions points to the need for new legislative power to cope with the problem. The 1961 report of the United States Civil Rights Commission recommended civil actions instituted in the name of the United States against state officials who conspire to exclude Negroes from juries. In order to accomplish this the Congress would need to pass legislation authorizing the Attorney General to institute such suits.

President Johnson's 1966 civil rights proposal contained a recommendation for new Federal legislation prohibiting racial discrimination in jury selection. Under the proposed legislation the Attorney General is authorized to bring a civil action in a Federal district court to ensure compliance by state and local courts. Furthermore, Federal courts may appoint a master to act as a jury official in situations where the Federal court finds it appropriate. If the proposal passes, it will probably not produce startling changes in Southern jury selections. An automatic trigger provision is needed. Under such a provision if a statistical history of a particular court indicated the probability of racial bias in selection, a Federal master would automatically be appointed.

"FOR A MAN'S HOME IS HIS CASTLE"

The history of American liberty is full of little paradoxes. One of the more instructive paradoxes in the development of the right against unreasonable searches and seizures concerns a great eighteenth-century empire builder and defender of liberty, William Pitt, Earl of Chatham. One of the most notable defenses of the sanctity of the home was made by Pitt:

> The poorest man may in his cottage bid defiance to all the forces of the Crown. It may be frail, its roof may shake; the wind may blow through it; the storms may enter,—the rain may enter,—but the King of England cannot enter. . . .

At the time of the famous John Wilkes case in the early 1760s, it was Pitt who led the opposition against the use of general warrants, warrants which were issued by the executive and which did not specify either the person or persons to be arrested or the places to be searched or the things to be seized.

Americans have a special fondness for this eighteenth-century giant. Pitt was one of the few true friends of the American colonists in the British government. When the colonists objected to the Stamp Act it was Pitt who said:

> I rejoice that America has resisted. Three millions of people, so dead to all the feelings of liberty, as voluntarily to submit to be slaves, would have been fit instruments to make slaves of the rest.

But Pitt, advocate of the American cause, foe of despotic government, was also a man who engaged in a long war with France to build the British Empire. Thus Pitt issued three general warrants in 1760 to apprehend French spies. In the same year Pitt, ironically, precipitated the colonial battle over the writs of assistance. In 1760, as principal minister of the Crown, he issued instructions to the colonial governors to prevent American trade with the French and to diligently enforce the acts of trade. The era of salutary neglect came to an end. But enforcement in face of the colonial smuggling trade meant the use of writs of assistance, writs similar in all respects to general warrants.

In looking back over the career of William Pitt, one might conclude that unrestricted power is safe in the hands of a man like Pitt, a man with a deep commitment to freedom, a man who strayed from the path of liberty only temporarily and then in the interests of a nation at war. It is easy to close one's eyes to the use of arbitrary powers to catch spies. But it was Pitt himself, in a sequel to the battle against general warrants, who said, "Unlimited power is apt to corrupt the minds of those who possess it." Free men cannot gamble their liberties

ex post facto that they have made a mistake, that they have proceeded against an innocent person.

Furthermore the argument ignores the reality of the problem of illegal searches and seizures. Within the past thirty years three national commissions have reported that unprofessional or undisciplined law-enforcement officers are insensitive to the Fourth Amendment.

Most of the violations are directed toward vagrants, drunkards, and maladjusted and economically underprivileged members of our society. An indication of the seriousness of the problem can be seen in a recent study done in the District of Columbia. In 1961 the District of Columbia Commissioners appointed a committee of lawyers to study police arrests in the district. The report was released in July, 1962, and revealed that the police had a policy of arresting on suspicion, or making so-called "investigatory" arrests. Such arrests are without prior probable cause and are clearly in violation of the Fourth Amendment. The report also revealed that relatively few persons detained for investigation were ever charged with a crime. The commissioners agreed to stop such arrests after March, 1963.

The proponents of the Weeks rule argue that it is the only practical deterrent against unreasonable searches and seizures by the police. By denying the police any benefit from an illegal search and seizure, it is felt that the rule discourages illegal enforcement of the law. The Weeks rule has been in effect on the Federal level for fifty years. There is little evidence to support the contention that it is an effective deterrent in preventing unreasonable searches and seizures in the majority of cases. It has its most effective force in the area of serious criminal offenses where the police are interested in bringing a prosecution; in dealing with petty crimes its remedial value is doubtful. If the police have no serious intention of prosecuting an individual they will not be constrained by a rule which can only be felt by denying them the use of illegal evidence in a prosecution. Additionally, the rule's effectiveness is dependent upon the police making an illegal seizure of articles which can then be returned to the defendant or suppressed as evidence. The exclusionary rule does not provide a remedy for an illegal arrest per se, unaccompanied by any incidental search and seizure. The testimony for this is found in the fact that for years the District of Columbia police felt free to make illegal arrests. The majority of arrests are not made with any intention of prosecution. The police look upon this illegal conduct in the area of petty crimes as a policy of harassment. They consider it a cheap and effective method of law enforcement.

The foregoing is not intended to imply that the rule should be abandoned. It is, however, a further indication of the limited ability of the judicial system to cope singlehandedly with social problems.

Aside from its limited remedial value the exclusionary rule has other justifications. From a moral viewpoint many people feel that the government should follow a policy of "clean hands" in criminal law enforcement; it should not stoop to the use of criminal tactics to enforce the law. Illegal enforcement of the law has a regressive element about it; it diminishes the respect for law in society.

There is some reason to believe that the deterrent value of the Weeks rule will be complemented in the future by tort actions against officers who commit unreasonable searches and seizures. Such action has been possible since the passage of the Civil Rights Act of 1871. Under this act any person who, under color of a state law, deprives a citizen of a federally protected right, is subject to an action for damages. Prior to 1961 the Federal courts repeatedly limited the scope of the action and for all practical purposes there was no possibility of proceeding under it. However, in 1961 the Supreme Court held that a Federal district court could hear such an action for damages based on an unreasonable search and seizure.[51] In December, 1962, the Federal district court jury awarded the aggrieved party $13,000 in damages. An award of $13,000 is enough to make police more cautious in invading privacy. Since the 1961 decision at least five actions have been filed in Federal courts against local officers for alleged unreasonable searches and seizures.[52]

The states and the exclusionary rule: Mapp v. Ohio. A further indication of the Court's concern about the problem of unreasonable searches and seizures is its recent extension of the Weeks rule to the states. By 1960, 26 states had adopted, in whole or in part, the Weeks rule. In 1961 in *Mapp v. Ohio* the Court applied the Weeks rule to the states.[53]

The *Mapp* case is the most ambitious decision of the Supreme Court in the field of state criminal justice. It is more ambitious than the rules applying to coerced confessions or counsel for defense in criminal cases. This is true because the *Mapp* case is attempting to influence the most widely used process in state criminal law: arrest, search, and seizure. By the Mapp rule the Court will be attempting to exert a de-

[51] *Monroe v. Pape,* 365 U.S. 167 (1961).
[52] For example, *Cox v. Shepherd,* 199 F. Supp. 140 (1961); defendants agreed to a stipulated judgment.
[53] *Mapp v. Ohio,* 367 U.S. 643 (1961).

gree of control over the out-of-court behavior of thousands of local police officers in every city and county across the United States.

It is perhaps because of the above reasons that the Court limited the impact of the *Mapp* case in a 1963 decision. In a California case the Court ruled that the Weeks rule of exclusion has a dual foundation; in part it is based on the Fourth Amendment and in part on the Supreme Court's general power to supervise the rules of evidence for Federal courts. The Court held that only that part of the Weeks rule which is based on the Fourth Amendment applies to the states as well as to the Federal government. In the particular case at hand, the Court allowed evidence to be admitted which the police had secured without a warrant by the simple expedient of getting the manager of an apartment to give the officers a key. The officers then walked into the occupied apartment totally unannounced. While this would be illegal on the Federal level, the Court indicated the states had greater latitude in criminal investigations.[54]

In limiting the impact of the *Mapp* decision the Court appears to be giving the states an opportunity to solve the problem of unreasonable invasions of privacy on a local or state level. However, the *Ker* decision can also invite disregard of reasonable process in criminal investigations. In September, 1963, four months after the *Ker* decision, the police of Riverside, California, smashed the door of a motel bedroom at 3 A.M. and arrested two sleeping men for a crime allegedly committed in Phoenix, Arizona. No arrest or search warrant was obtained. It is doubtful whether a California court could have issued a warrant for an Arizona offense.

That fugitives from justice should be apprehended and tried is not disputed but whether the police should be allowed to smash bedroom doors at 3 A.M. without a warrant is at least open to question. In this case, as in thousands of others, the judicial protection of privacy was totally ineffective. Let us assume *arguendo*, that the men were guilty of the Phoenix crime. Society has an important stake in apprehending such fugitives. To this end the quickest and cheapest method was used by the Riverside police. Let us further assume here that all the policemen involved were men of good will. But unfortunately the "most reliable" information can turn out to be false, and men of good will do make mistakes. The *Ker* decision invites men of good will with "reliable information" to make mistakes, mistakes which invade the constitutional privacy of innocent persons.

[54] *Ker v. California,* 83 Sup. Ct. 1623 (1963).

On the night of November 14, 1963, a young Riverside couple and their children were asleep in their apartment, when the wife was awakened by someone attempting to enter the apartment. The wife then awakened her husband and the husband seized an unloaded rifle. The persons attempting to enter the apartment flashed a light into the window and when they saw the husband holding a rifle they fired two shots into the apartment. They then smashed down the door of the apartment and entered. The men were officers of the Riverside city police. The eight officers searched the apartment and arrested the husband.

The November 14 incident began with the robbery of a service station earlier that same night. A patrolman, who had a description of the robber, was making a routine check of a bar. He asked a patron of the bar if he had seen a man fitting the description of the robber. The patron said he had and that in fact the suspect had asked him to drive him to a nearby apartment and the patron had done so. Unfortunately, the patron led the police to the wrong apartment house, an apartment house outside the city limits of Riverside. From this point on, a routine investigation turned into a bizarre affair. "Reliable information" in the hands of overly enthusiastic policemen endangered the lives of an innocent and unsuspecting family, the privacy of a home was invaded, and a husband was arrested for brandishing a weapon.[55]

After the arrest the suspect was taken to the service station where the attendant said that he was not the robber. However, the police held the man until late the next morning. The police then made a statement that the officers had been justified in doing all they had done.

There is certainly grave doubt whether a reasonable and prudent man would have considered the uncorroborated tip of a bar patron as probable cause for dispensing with a warrant and breaking into the home of a person totally unknown to the officers in an area outside of the limits of the city. Yet the *Ker* decision, paralleling the Riverside incident in many respects, invites law-enforcement officers to take such actions.

In the last analysis one can take little comfort in shifting responsibility for the control of unreasonable criminal procedures to the judiciary. The proper solution in most situations is broadly a political one.

[55] In February, 1964, Riverside police admitted placing a choke hold on a narcotics suspect who was allegedly attempting to swallow heroin. Police later took the suspect to a hospital and forcefully pumped his stomach. Cf. *Rochin v. California*, 342 U.S. 165 (1952), where the Supreme Court described similar conduct as shocking to the conscience.

It begins with ensuring that police departments have budgets adequate for the enforcement of law *and* the protection of individual liberties. A police force of adequate size, training, and facilities need not take short cuts in law enforcement. Where the budget is adequate and the police do take short cuts which jeopardize individual liberties, then city councils, political parties, churches, labor unions, and bar associations should be alert to these violations and bring pressure on the police to reform their practices. The price of liberty, thus, is a vigilant but not a stingy citizenry.

Review Questions

1. Have you observed in your community any serious increase in crime? If so, would you attribute this to the procedural limitations placed on the police? If not, to what would you attribute the increase?

2. What is the McNabb-Mallory rule? What is the Weeks rule? Do you feel these rules are overly solicitous of the person accused of crime?

3. Does a Negro have a right to have a member of his race as a juror in a criminal trial against him? Can you recall any trial in your community where a Negro served on the jury?

4. Would you support legislation to allow a system of judicial or court-ordered wiretapping? Give your reasons.

5. What is the subjective test of coercion in confession cases? Do you know whether it is the practice of the police in your community to question suspects prior to arraignment?

THE IDEAL
OF LIBERTY

Chapter 6

AMERICA: AN EMPIRE OF LIBERTY

The poets of America testify to the insight of Walt Whitman's line, "I hear America singing, the varied carols I hear." America is Carl Sandburg singing:

> Hog Butcher for the World
> Tool Maker, Stacker of Wheat.

It is the ragtime beat of Vachel Lindsay's

> Wild crap-shooters with a whoop and a call
> Danced the juba in their gambling hall,

and the blues of Langston Hughes's

> Clean the spittoons boy.
> Detroit
> Chicago
> Atlantic City
> Palm Beach.

It is the bitterness of John Dos Passos'

> enie menie minie moe plenty of other
> pine boxes stacked up there containing
> what they'd scraped up of Richard Roe.

America is Robert Frost's quiet love of the land:

> Whose woods these are I think I know
> His house is in the village though;
> He will not see me stopping here
> To watch his woods fill up with snow.

And America is the promise of Joel Barlow's *The Columbiad:*

> Here social man a second birth shall find
> And a new range of reason lift his mind,
> Feed his strong intellect with pure light,
> A nobler sense of duty and of right,
> The sense of liberty. . . .

The Columbiad reflected the promise of America as a free nation in the early part of the nineteenth century. Barlow published his poem in 1807 when his friend Thomas Jefferson was President. Both Barlow and Jefferson shared the same hopeful vision of America.

America has been varied carols—it has been ragtime, blues and bitterness; it has been a "city of big shoulders" and a land of snow-covered woods. But towering above all else America has been a vision of liberty. Jefferson called it "an empire of liberty." In his First Inaugural Address he spoke of "a rising nation, spread over a wide and fruitful land." And to Jefferson the heart and soul of that nation was its dedication to liberty. He had indeed so dedicated our nation when he wrote:

> We hold these truths to be self-evident, that all men
> are created equal, that they are endowed by their

Creator with certain unalienable Rights, that among
these are Life, Liberty and the pursuit of Happiness.

Jefferson realized that a national dedication to liberty meant little
without a personal commitment to the ideal. Jefferson made such a
commitment. In 1800 he wrote to Benjamin Rush, "I have sworn upon
the altar of God eternal hostility against every form of tyranny over
the mind of man." Jefferson was not always true to his own high
principles, nor has America always been true to Jefferson. Yet America
still reflects Jefferson's optimism, his hopeful view of man. He wrote to
Pierre Du Pont de Nemours in 1816, "I believe with you that morality,
compassion, generosity are innate elements of the human spirit."

Much of Jefferson's program is dated, but as Lincoln observed, his
principles remain "the definition and axioms of a free society." A personal dedication to liberty, a belief in the essential goodness and moral
capacity of man—these were the principles of Jefferson and they remain
the principles of all free societies.

THE THREE CONSTITUTIONS OF LIBERTY

While Jefferson's principles help each generation of Americans to re-
affirm its belief in individual liberty, nonetheless Jefferson cannot solve
for each generation the problem of relating liberty to time. To para-
phrase Clinton Rossiter, we see as far as we do because we stand on
the shoulders of men like Jefferson. But we cannot look to the past
for solutions. The conflicts in civil liberties must be solved by each
generation. The ideal of liberty is always more or less in the balance
in our law and in our social order.

Aristotle described a constitution as a "way of life of a citizen-body."
He also described three "right" constitutions and the conditions under
which they thrive and the conditions leading to their perversion. In a
broad sense this book has been dealing with three constitutions and the
discord in these constitutions. If a constitution is a way of life followed
by a citizen-body, then the ideal constitution is the best possible life
for that citizen-body. An ideal constitution is based on certain ethical
or moral principles, particularly as they relate to the relationships between man and the state.

In democratic theory the principal ideal is liberty and the claimant
is moral man. But liberty as an abstraction becomes meaningful only
when we relate liberty in time to its component parts. In this book we
have been concerned with a few of the subsidiary ideals which stem

from liberty: equality, privacy, and independence or freedom from external restraints in religion, speech, and press. These abstractions have been accepted in democratic theory in what can be described as a "constitution of ideals." But a constitution of ideals may or may not be in harmony with a second constitution which we shall call a "constitution of laws." By this we mean a written document called *The* Constitution, and the statutes of legislative bodies, and the great body of rules called the common law. The law should give expression to the "constitution of ideals." It is the *should* or *ought* of the law that is so frequently missing in the analysis of issues in civil liberties. We can examine the "rules" as laid down by legislatures and the courts and give a fair approximation of what the law "is." But whether the law satisfies our ideals and our society is another matter. In examining current issues we need to judge the "law" in the wider context of our basic moral assumptions about liberty in society.

Finally, we have a third constitution which is best described as a "constitution of the community," which should practice our ideals as expressed in the law. The community, or sometimes the communities, acts upon and reacts to both our democratic ideals and our law. For example, freedom of the press is an ideal expressed in the law, but as seen in the chapter on obscenity and censorship the community reacts to freedom of the press in varying degrees of harmony and discord. A particular community's response to censorship is dependent on certain broad national cultural trends, which in turn are the results of the changing environment.

Industrialization and the changing position of the family influenced literary trends and made sex a more acceptable subject in literature. The law gradually reflected the changes. Yet in certain communities the wider literary freedom and the consequent changes in the law may or may not be accepted. Acceptance here is dependent to a large degree on certain conditions in the community, e.g., the degree of contact with wider cultural influences, the position of higher education, the status of the local press, and even on such transitory local problems as the crime rate.

There need be no implication from the foregoing that the three constitutions are in a constant discord. There are areas where there is a happy conjunction of the three constitutions. The ideal of freedom of religious belief, the unalienable right of man to approach or not to approach God, is one such conjunction. Our law, as expressed in the First Amendment, in the various state constitutions, and in the statutes and the judicial interpretations of these documents, gives clear expression to this ideal. And in communities across the nation this ideal, this law, is practiced. In general in the United States one may believe or not believe in God. The discord at the current time appears on the local level when a community forces God into the public classroom.

When we turn from the ideal of freedom of religious belief to the ideal of freedom of religious practice we find discord more likely to appear. Take, for example, the aggressive proselytizing activities of the Jehovah's Witnesses in the 1930s. The right to proselytize is a legally recognized part of the liberty of religious bodies. Yet in numerous communities in the United States the Jehovah's Witnesses were denied this right. Today this body is able to conduct its religious activities in far greater freedom than twenty years ago. In part this can be attributed to the greater restraint exercised today by individual Jehovah's Witnesses in proselytizing. But perhaps more influential than this is the fact that religious freedom is more widely accepted today on a national level and in turn is reflected in community practice.

Continuing in the religious area, when we turn to separation of church and state we see an even greater degree of discord in the three constitutions. The basic explanation for this is that the "ideal" of separation of church and state is not deeply rooted in America. Its initial acceptance in the "law" was by means of the no establishment clause of the First Amendment. Yet the ideal behind this clause was liberty of religious belief and practice and not separation for the sake of separation. Based on the experience of earlier times it was thought that union of church and state would endanger freedom of religious belief and practice. There is still consensus on this point in the United States and no establishment is a reality. However, neither the law nor the society is fully convinced that the neo-Jeffersonian idea of separation of church and state is an ideal that should be accepted. Many fail to see how the ideal of liberty of religious belief or practice is endangered by a program of limited aid to parochial schools. It may well be that the neo-Jeffersonian concept of separation is being pressed as an ideal type when its intrinsic value for liberty in our generation has yet to be established.

EQUALITY AND THE THREE CONSTITUTIONS

Equality is one of Western civilizations's oldest ideals. It is a part of liberty. The Greek Stoics gave Western civilization the ethical principle of the equality of man before the state. The early Stoic concept of equality was based on the belief that the divine spark of reason is common to the nature of man. The Stoics reasoned that this common bond of humanity, applying equally to all men—free, slave, foreigner, and barbarian—made it necessary that at least in certain areas the state should be no respecter of persons. Christianity incorporated the ideal of equality. St. Paul wrote, "You are neither Greek nor Jew, bond nor slave, for you are all one in Christ Jesus." And Jefferson wrote, "We hold these truths to be self-evident, that all men are created equal. . . ." Pope John XXIII wrote in 1963 in his encyclical *Pacem in Terris:*

> Human society is realized in freedom, that is to say, in ways and means in keeping with the dignity of its citizens, who accept the responsibility of their actions, precisely because they are by nature rational beings.

Equality as one of the component parts of liberty means that there is no privileged class before the law; that in the courts, in the legislatures, or in the police stations or schools all men stand on an equal footing. The ideal means that there is neither black nor white, rich nor poor, Christian nor Jew, but only moral man, each having an equal claim to dignity and respect. The ideal finds countless expressions in our law. The Fourteenth Amendment holds that "no state shall deny to any person the equal protection of the laws." And the courts have generally stated that this means equal laws equally administered.

The most glaring note of discord in equality today is the position of the Negro in America. At least until the present, the white man has been privileged and the law and society have treated the Negro on a different basis than the white. The explanation for this, at least in part, can be attributed to the belief that the Negro was indeed inferior and thus not a rightful claimant to equality. What was so obvious to all was the cultural lag of the Negro. What was forgotten was the fact that there is more that unites white and black than separates them. They share a common moral capacity and common human dignity.

As these bonds were realized by increasingly large numbers of persons, particularly after the 1920s, the Negro began to be accepted as a rightful claimant to the ideal of equality. Once the claim to the ideal was recognized, then the law began to change. The courts and later the legislative bodies attempted to bring the law into harmony with the ideal. Nonetheless, there are still many communities where the Negro is considered an inferior, where the Negro shares neither in the ideal nor in the law of equality. What we are witnessing today is an appeal by the Negro not to the law because the "law" has only been partially successful in changing the community, but rather an appeal to the conscience of the community. The appeal is intended to open the hearts of Northerners and Southerners to the Judaic-Christian principle of the brotherhood of man.

THE THREE CONSTITUTIONS: THE PROCESS OF HARMONY

The Negro revolt is also illustrative of another aspect of the civil liberties scene in America. When the constitution of the community, when the community practice, is in basic discord with the constitution of ideals, then the first appeal for harmony is generally to the constitution of laws. The Negro, with notable lack of success, appeals to a school board, the sheriff, or the registrar of voters that a certain discriminatory practice is in violation of the "law." He attempts to persuade the official to reconcile practice with the law. Naturally this process of conflict resolution assumes that channels of communications exist and can be used. Yet one of the most basic problems the Negro faces, particularly in the South, is lack of communication with the white community. The Albany Movement's first step was an attempt to establish communication with the city commissioners. They failed and then they appealed the "law" to the courts.

It is interesting to note that it is frequently observed that our courts are the last and basic protectors of civil liberties. All that can be meant by this is that the courts do attempt to reconcile ideals, the law, and community practices. In some areas the judiciary assumes an initial burden in preserving liberty. In the area of criminal procedures the courts have established a variety of rules, such as the rule against the use of illegally obtained evidence, aimed at securing liberty. But judicial protection of liberty assumes a degree of direct confrontation and conflict between the individual and the state, e.g., an arrest. Yet liberty is not always endangered by such open conflicts. The Negro is not always denied the right to vote by means of an obvious discrimination which a court of law can remedy. The denial may be by means of subtle intimidation. In such cases the courts can only give limited relief. Even where there is sufficient admissible evidence to grant injunctive relief, new forms of intimidation can be invented. The Negro then discovers that the judicial solution must be complemented with an additional tactic.

The political versus the judicial resolution. In the preface of this book it was stated that liberty is not essentially a legal matter. Liberty is partly a legal matter—rules do play a significant and desirable part in the preservation of liberty. But there is in the United States an almost Germanic tendency, in part fostered by the judiciary, to escape the more difficult political process for the judicial process. Yet the courts are by no means the best protectors of liberty. The Negro today recognizes this and he has enlarged his strategy to include a political resolution of desegregation.

There is common agreement among friends and foes of the *Brown* decision that it would have been better if the Congress had decided the issue and not the Supreme Court. Had Congress written legislation in 1954 to accomplish the same ends as the *Brown* decision this would have inevitably brought a vast number of people into closer connection with desegregation. Local party committees, candidates, and pressure groups would have become involved to a greater degree and far earlier than they did under the *Brown* decision. The implication for the future is that conflict resolution in civil liberties should become more political and less judicial. Yet this lesson of the *Brown* decision seems to be lost.

In 1963 the Senate passed a bill which included a provision allowing a Federal taxpayer to bring a suit in the Federal District Court in the District of Columbia to test the constitutionality of the disbursement of Federal monies to sectarian colleges under college loan legislation. As mentioned in Chapter 4, church-related colleges have been receiving low-interest building loans from the Federal government since the 1950s. The intent of the 1963 Senate amendment was to test the "constitutionality" of these loans with a view to settling the issue of separation of church and state, at least in this one area. Aside from the constitutionally questionable procedure of inviting test cases, the amendment presumes that Federal aid to sectarian institutions is a legal issue. Merely "passing the buck" to the courts does not alter the political nature of the question. No matter which way the courts would decide the issue, at least at this juncture of American history, the outcome would be unacceptable to a large segment of the American people. If this issue is ripe for resolution, the churches, schools and colleges, the political parties, and the Congress must solve it and not the courts.

When we turn to criminal justice we are faced with a similar problem. At the present time criminal justice is viewed as essentially a legal problem. But when we examine the problem of coerced confessions we are not viewing just a legal problem. The practice of obtaining coerced confessions, just like the practice of making illegal searches and seizures, frequently has an economic foundation—the lack of adequate budgetary support and the consequent pressures to take short cuts in enforcing the criminal law. The solution to this is political and not judicial. And a political solution to issues in civil liberties means that parties and pressure groups—churches, unions, bar associations, and corporations—must assume their full civic responsibilities. Rousseau told us that freedom is a burdensome responsibility.

The appeal to the conscience. When the political solution to the Negro issue fell short of resolving the conflict, the Negro made a third appeal. He began sit-ins and demonstrations in order to appeal to the conscience of the nation. To say that this appeal, through what Martin Luther King has called "creative tension," is to the conscience of the nation is to acknowledge that emotions will play a significant role in the appeal. And it must be further acknowledged that an emotional appeal is to some extent a flight from reason.

There is certainly a place for rationalistic discussion in the Negro issue. Evidence, for example, can be assembled about the economic consequences of race discrimination, particularly as it has affected the labor market. To some extent this appeal has had an impact in the South. The business community in Atlanta has been influenced somewhat by such an approach. But this approach alone does not offer hope for a comprehensive solution in either the North or the South. Not everyone can be reached in this fashion. But many Negro leaders evidently do feel that a very large segment of the population can be reached by an appeal to the moral issue.

An assumption of the moral approach is that the segregationist shares with the Negro a belief in the essential goodness and moral capacity of all men. But if the segregationist does not share this belief—if he believes, on the contrary, that the Negro has the curse of Chanaan on him—then the appeal to the conscience will fail. Whether there is an appeal beyond the conscience of man is an explosive question which should make black and white pause.

The foregoing analysis could be developed further to include the ideals of privacy, or freedom of speech and press, or fundamental fairness in criminal justice. However, the above analysis is sufficient to illustrate that the problem for liberty is how to achieve a harmony of our ideals, our laws, and our daily lives. This harmony can only be attained when we are individually committed to and have a faith in freedom.

THE LIMITS OF LIBERTY

Faith in freedom is not faith in license. Aristotle observed that "most men find more pleasure in living without any discipline than they find in a life of temperance." A belief in self-discipline and temperance is as necessary for the preservation of liberty as a belief in the moral capacity of man. While the ideal of liberty stands out as the most fundamental part of democratic values, it is, nevertheless, in competition with other values.

The Preamble to the Constitution is a statement of the problem we face as much as it is a preamble.

> We the people of the United States, in order to form a more perfect Union, establish justice, insure domestic tranquility, provide for the common defense, promote the general welfare and secure the blessings of liberty to ourselves and our Posterity, do ordain and establish this Constitution for the United States of America.

Here in the Preamble liberty is in competition with the preservation of the Union, domestic tranquility, the common defense, and the general welfare. For example, liberty was sacrificed during the Civil War to the cause of Union; freedom of assembly must be reconciled with community order; the rights of private property must be adjusted to the general welfare; and freedom of speech can take on a more limited dimension where the nation's security is involved.

John Stuart Mill wrote, "The practical question [is] where to place the limit—how to make the fitting adjustment between individual independence and social control." There is no formula for making "the fitting adjustment." But when we attempt to make the adjustment we should be aware that the only meaningful liberty exists in society and this in turn means that liberties carry with them responsibilities to society.

The resolution of conflicts in liberty will be made less difficult when the individual's belief in liberty carries with it a commitment to liberty for all other individuals. We need to recall that our essential goodness and moral capacity are shared by our neighbors. Furthermore, our faith in liberty must include an attitude of self-examination and a willingness to hear the pleas of others. What we may assume to be our liberty may be another man's serfdom.

The exercise of liberty does not require that all the participants be gentlemen; however, it does require that each participant recognize his adversary as a man. Liberty entitles one to hold a position firmly and fervently in the face of prevailing opinion; it does not entitle one to become a political gladiator. Liberty cannot survive in an arena of hate; it can only survive where the actions of a man are widened by the horizon of humanity.

For Further Reading

BARTH, ALAN: *Government by Investigations*, The Viking Press, Inc., New York, 1955.

BETH, LOREN: *The American Theory of Church and State*, University of Florida Press, Gainesville, Fla., 1958.

CHAFEE, ZECHARIAH: *Free Speech in the United States*, Harvard University Press, Cambridge, Mass., 1954.

COGLEY, JOHN (ed.): *Religion in America*, Meridian Books, Inc., New York, 1958.

DASH, SAM: *The Eavesdroppers*, Rutgers University Press, New Brunswick, N.J., 1959.

DONNER, FRANK J.: *The Un-Americans*, Ballantine Books, Inc., New York, 1962.

DRAPER, THEODORE: *The Roots of American Communism*, The Viking Press, Inc., New York, 1957.

FELLMAN, DAVID: *The Defendant's Rights*, Holt, Rinehart and Winston, Inc., New York, 1958.

HANEY, ROBERT W.: *Comstockery in America*, Beacon Press, Boston, 1960.

HEALEY, ROBERT M.: *Jefferson on Religion in Public Education*, Yale University Press, New Haven, Conn., 1962.

INGLIS, RUTH A.: *Freedom of the Movies*, The University of Chicago Press, Chicago, 1947.

JANSON, DONALD, and BERNARD EISMANN: *The Far Right*, McGraw-Hill Book Company, New York, 1963.

KURLAND, PHILIP B.: *Religion and the Law*, Aldine Publishing Co., London, 1963.

MCKEON, RICHARD, *et al.*: *The Freedom to Read*, R. R. Bowker Company, New York, 1957.

MAGUIRE, JOHN: *Evidence of Guilt: Restrictions upon Its Discovery or Compulsory Disclosure*, Little, Brown and Company, Boston, 1959.

MYRDAL, GUNNAR, *et al.*: *An American Dilemma*, Harper & Row, Publishers, Incorporated, New York, 1944.

O'NEILL, JAMES M.: *Catholicism and American Freedom*, Harper & Row, Publishers, Incorporated, New York, 1952.

PACKER, HERBERT L.: *Ex-communist Witnesses*, Stanford University Press, Stanford, Calif., 1962.

ROCK, JOHN: *The Time Has Come: A Catholic Doctor's Proposals to End the Battle over Birth Control,* Alfred A. Knopf, Inc., New York, 1963.

SHANNON, DAVID A.: *The Decline of American Communism,* Harcourt, Brace & World, Inc., New York, 1959.

STOKES, ANSON P.: *Church and State in the United States,* Yale University Press, New Haven, Conn., 1949.

TUMIN, MELVIN, *et al.: Desegregation: Resistance and Readiness,* Princeton University Press, Princeton, N.J., 1958.

UNITED STATES COMMISSION ON CIVIL RGHTS: 1961 Report, Books 1–5, *Voting, Education, Housing, Justice, Employment,* U.S. Government Printing Office, 1961.

Index